HOW WE READ THE BIBLE

HOW WE READ THE
BIBLE

A Guide to Scripture's Style and Meaning

Karolien Vermeulen
Elizabeth R. Hayes

WILLIAM B. EERDMANS PUBLISHING COMPANY
GRAND RAPIDS, MICHIGAN

Wm. B. Eerdmans Publishing Co.
4035 Park East Court SE, Grand Rapids, Michigan 49546
www.eerdmans.com

Book design by Leah Luyk

Printed in the United States of America

28 27 26 25 24 23 22   2 3 4 5 6 7

ISBN 978-0-8028-7809-0

Library of Congress Cataloging-in-Publication Data

Names: Vermeulen, Karolien, author. | Hayes, Elizabeth R. (Elizabeth Russell),
    1952– author.
Title: How we read the Bible : a guide to scripture's style and meaning /
    Karolien Vermeulen, Elizabeth R. Hayes.
Description: Grand Rapids, Michigan : William B. Eerdmans Publishing
    Company, 2022. | Includes bibliographical references and index. | Summary:
    "A handbook on reading the Bible that explores the interaction between the
    cues of the text and the context of the reader through key stylistic ele-
    ments"—Provided by publisher.
Identifiers: LCCN 2021055325 | ISBN 9780802878090 (paperback)
Subjects: LCSH: Bible—Criticism, interpretation, etc. | Bible—Language, style.
    | Bible—Hermeneutics. | BISAC: RELIGION / Biblical Studies / Exegesis &
    Hermeneutics | LITERARY CRITICISM / Ancient & Classical
Classification: LCC BS511.3 .V475 2022 | DDC 220.6—dc23/eng/20220126
LC record available at https://lccn.loc.gov/2021055325

Contents

III THE PROCESS OF READING A TEXT

List of Abbreviations

AIL	Ancient Israel and Its Literature
BZAW	Beihefte zur Zeitschrift für die alttestamentliche Wissenschaft
CSLI	Center for the Study of Language and Information
KJV	King James Version
NASB	New American Standard Bible
NIV	New International Version
NRSV	New Revised Standard Version
Strong's	*Strong's Exhaustive Concordance of the Bible*
LN	Louw-Nida numbers
v(v).	verse(s)
JSOTSup	Journal for the Study of the Old Testament Supplement Series
LHBOTS	The Library of Hebrew Bible/Old Testament Studies

On How We Read the Bible and Why We Need to Know It

When we speak of reading the *Bible*, specifically of *how* we read the Bible as the title of this book suggests, a few questions immediately come to mind. For example, which Bible are we reading: The Hebrew Bible? The New Testament? A word-for-word English translation such as the NASB? A dynamic equivalent version such as the NIV? Any of the myriad other "first language" translations such as the *Elberfelder Bibel* in German or the *Statenvertaling* in Dutch, Bible versions suitable for reading in one's mother tongue? Is the Apocrypha in or out? Are we reading the Bible as a sample of ancient Hebrew or Greek language, as literature, or as the inspired word of God?

Clearly *how* we read the Bible is predicated on the variety of preferences, presuppositions, and contexts surrounding the readers themselves. Some readers will see the text as Holy Scripture, others as Holy Scripture presented as literature, yet others as a series of good stories intermixed with history, poetry, and wisdom. Thus, it is necessary to acknowledge that reading the Bible is a process that involves both the chosen text and the reader—and to recognize that readers come fully equipped with certain presuppositions, different ranges of linguistic skills, and unique memories, feelings, and emotions. Or as Craig C. Broyles has put it more sharply, "The first subject for the interpretation of the Bible is [thus] not the Bible, but the interpreter" (2001, 16). With this sentence, Broyles draws attention to the role of the reader and the interaction between reader and text in the interpretive process. This volume looks at the way readers, the world they live in, and the text work together to make meaning. In this way, the rather broad term "we" in the title is not monolithic. Each reader is invited to locate themselves within their own context. For *how* we read the Bible is often colored by *why* we read the Bible.

The How of Reading

Reading and the Bible are two peas in a pod. They seem to be natural partners. However, the why of reading has received far more attention over time than the how of reading. Biblical theology, history, law, rituals, and worldviews have all been studied extensively. Even philology, the science of the word, wondered about why a form was "a rather than b" or why certain parts of the Bible use later forms of Hebrew or loanwords from other languages. For an answer to the question "How do we make sense of the biblical text?" we have to wait until the 1970s and 1980s when *literary approaches* made their way into the field of biblical studies. Scholars such as Meir Weiss (1984) and Robert Alter (1980, 1985) broke the ground for reading the (Hebrew) Bible as literature. They introduced key parts of storytelling, such as characters, time, place, plot, and perspective and applied them to the biblical text. They also paid attention to "special" language, stylized uses of language that draw readers' attention, such as unusual images or repetitions. Weiss, Alter, and many others with them offered tools to untangle how a text is composed. However, they left out an important player, that is, the reader. In the end, the reader is the one who construes the characters, the time, and each of the other story elements in their mind. What is more, the "special" language, which has given the text the label "literary" before, turns out to be just language, put in a specific way in order to influence how we read the text. Understanding Bible reading is not just studying the story elements that make up the puzzle of a narrative; it is also considering the piecing together of these elements as you go through a text. This process is the object of study of a field called *cognitive stylistics*. It shares concerns with literary approaches, but also focuses on things beyond that field. The label *cognitive* refers to the fact that this field is interested in what happens in the mind. How do we go from singular words to envisioning a text world? Which processes allow us, human beings, to imagine story worlds just by looking at words in a text? The term *stylistics* indicates that the field looks for its answers in the style of the text, in how its words are put together, which words are chosen, and what they evoke. Style is much more than a handful of rhetorical devices. It is the form of a text more generally, which is taken as a guide for reading. Thus, form includes both the language studied by linguists—you will finally find out why grammar matters!—and by literary scholars—no worries, we will still pay attention to beautiful metaphors and ingenious plot twists.

One of the main assets of stylistics is its interest in the variety in interpretation due to the difference in readers and their contexts, as pointed out above. Simultaneously, however, this variety comes with a uniformity as far as reading processes go. Whereas readers may have various reasons to turn to the Bible, the act of reading itself always follows similar pathways. Precisely, therefore, this book focuses on the elements that make up this reading process. You will notice that many of the items discussed sound vaguely familiar. They are easy to understand and to apply because they come naturally with the act of reading, regardless of the kind of text that is read. The fact that we, as readers, are human beings creates a common ground for reading the biblical text. This immediately brings us to a second advantage of the suggested approach: this manual can assist in reading the Bible in various contexts and for a plethora of reasons. As a method, stylistics is easily combined with other frameworks, such as literary readings, theological analyses, historical studies, and so on. Finally, the book acknowledges the biblical text in all its complexity: as a text with different audiences over time, as a piece of literature, as an ideology, as a discourse, and as a text with specific features such as parallelism or traces of orality.

The How of This Book

The volume consists of three parts. It starts with the basic building blocks of reading texts, then moves to covering mid-level elements that require connections between the basic items, and concludes with features that assist in unravelling larger text fragments. Each chapter explains the introduced concepts and illustrates them with biblical examples. After a short history of where the concept stems from, a connection is made with precedents or comparable discussions in previous biblical research. Furthermore, a larger piece of text serves as a case study to show how and in which cases the new concept can be useful for reading the Bible. The case study is followed by ideas for discussion, which include text passages and guiding questions. A section with suggestions for further reading concludes each chapter. Full references of works mentioned under "Further Reading" can be found in the bibliography.

In part 1, the focus is on basic concepts that are present in all texts. Chapter 1 begins with a discussion of words as being part of larger word fields that are evoked when a *word of the field* is used in a text. In chapter 2, the notion of *categories* is introduced. When we process text, we constantly categorize the information based on knowledge we already have. This categorization happens for simple words, such as "son," but also when we decide on the genre of a story or biblical book, for example. Another key feature for reading is the play with attention and focus, discussed in chapter 3. Some elements in a text draw our attention, others do not. The former is called a figure, the latter is called the ground.[1] Figures can be created in various ways, for example, with repetition or rare words. Neither figures nor grounds are fixed; they move as the story progresses. The same mobility can be noticed with perspective in stories. Who is speaking and whose viewpoint are we taking? These are the central questions of chapter 4. Part 1 ends with chapter 5 on *cognitive grammar*, as the first step to combine words and to move to a mid-level category of processing. *Grammar* is the way in which words are put together according to certain rules.

Part 2 draws on the basic concepts introduced in part 1 by a discussion of mid-level features that are no longer identifiable in the text as such but are triggered in the mind by specific words and structures in the text. In chapter 6, for example, schemas and *scripts* form the focus of attention. The mentioning of a table, food, and people in a text will activate a SUPPER schema.[2] This schema in our mind also has other attributes to it, such as drinks, music, perhaps, or singing. The text does not need to specify these other items. What is more, when the text introduces something that is not in the schema in our mind, we will be surprised, and when something that we are expecting is missing, we may be disappointed or taken aback. Chapter 7 introduces *mental spaces* as knowledge structures that are constructed when thinking and talking. For example, the phrase "we are writing this book from home in 2020" would be our base space. When we then say that we had not imagined a home birth for this book, we introduce a second mental space. What is more, we are blending our base space of writing at home (rather than in the office or together at a coffee bar) with this second mental space of giving birth at home. The *blended space* includes traits from both the base space of writing and the new space of home birthing. This connection-making process is central in two other features that are discussed in chapters 8 and 9. In chapter 8 we look at metaphor and how our mind connects similar concepts. As a result, we have no problem reading about God the shepherd or Jerusalem the woman. Chapter 9 focuses on metonymy and how already like elements are connected. In these cases, we are reading about happy hearts rather than happy people and

---

1. Words appearing in the glossary are in bold in the first occurrence in each chapter in which they appear.

2. All knowledge structures mentioned in part 2 (schemas, mental spaces, conceptual metaphors, and conceptual metonymies) will appear in small caps, following the convention in cognitive linguistics.

mercy from heaven rather than from God. Once more, our reading brains have little difficulty making these connections. Yet, paying attention to such things more closely tells us a lot about reading and understanding the Bible, which is precisely what this book wants to offer.

Part 3 then turns to concepts that play on the level of larger text fragments and the Bible as a whole. As the features in part 2 drew on the concepts discussed in part 1, the concepts found in part 3 draw on all of the concepts discussed in parts 1 and 2. It may have become clear by now that reading may seem like a simple task but it actually involves a lot of underlying work. In chapter 10, we look at discourse worlds, the immediate situational context surrounding the reading of a text. The most important things to take away from this chapter are that (1) discourse worlds are more than historical-theological background knowledge but also include beliefs, dreams, and feelings of writers and readers; and (2) the biblical text has a split discourse world, meaning that the immediate context of the writers and original readers of the text is different from that of later readers, including the modern ones. In addition to the text-external world discussed in chapter 10, chapters 11 and 12 pay attention to the text-internal world. Chapter 11 focuses on possible worlds and how texts include images of worlds that will never be realized. It shows how possible worlds make for a more challenging and interesting reading experience and how the reader plays a role in that as well. Finally, chapter 12, which is about text worlds, brings all the previous chapters together in a reading method that considers reading to be an act of world building. It points out which elements in a text assist in this creative process, demonstrates where the reader and his world enter, and illustrates how all of this gives us better insight into the biblical text.

At Last

We conceptualize this book as a reading tool. There is no single way of using it. Whereas it makes sense to start at the beginning with the basic building blocks and end with text worlds as the chapter in which everything comes together, there are other ways to work with it as well. For example, the elements discussed in part 2 are all knowledge structures, categories in the mind. If you start there, you can consequently consider on which smaller concepts they draw (part 1) as well as to which bigger ideas they lead (part 3). Another way to use this book is to start at the very end, where the text is approached holistically, to turn to each of the smaller elements as they appear in the analysis.

And of course, you are welcome to select any topics of your interest or biblical books that are discussed, sampling from the book rather than reading it cover to cover.

As should have been clear by now, *How We Read the Bible* is not prescriptive. It will not tell you how to read the Bible, let alone why to read it. Rather, it gives you directions that can be found in the text, cues to pay attention to, and insight into the underlying processes that make up reading the Bible text. At every moment it considers your role as a reader. In the end, you decide how and why to read your Bible.

Further Reading

The quote in the second paragraph can be found in Craig C. Broyles's book *Interpreting the Old Testament: A Guide for Exegesis* (2001).

Two key figures in the literary reading of the Hebrew Bible are Meir Weiss and Robert Alter. Weiss's earlier work in Hebrew was made available in English in *The Bible from Within: The Method of Total Interpretation* (1984). Robert Alter wrote two accessible introductions to biblical narrative and poetry with *The Art of Biblical Narrative* (1980) and *The Art of Biblical Poetry* (1985). Various other introductions followed. To name just a few, Michael Fishbane, *Biblical Text and Texture: A Literary Reading of Selected Texts* (1979); Robert Alter and Frank Kermode, eds., *The Literary Guide to the Bible* (1978); Adele Berlin, *Poetics and Interpretation of Biblical Narrative* (1983); and David M. Gunn and Danna Nolan Fewell, *Narrative in the Hebrew Bible* (1993).

For the New Testament, the following works can be consulted: Norman Petersen, *Literary Criticism for New Testament Critics* (1978); Alan R. Culpepper, *Anatomy of the Fourth Gospel: A Study in Literary Design* (1983); and Robert Tannehill, *The Narrative Unity of Luke-Acts: A Literary Interpretation* (1986, 1990).

PART ONE

The Bits and Pieces of Reading

ONE

Words in Context

Building Blocks of Meaning

What Happens as We Read

Meaning is created as we read, word upon word, clause upon clause, line upon line, paragraph upon paragraph. While reading appears to be a linear process, it is by no means straightforward. This running process calls upon our stored, **encyclopedic background knowledge** of the world. This knowledge base includes factual knowledge, along with our emotions, thoughts, and feelings. The process may be slowed when we run across an unfamiliar term or turn of phrase, requiring a quick check in a dictionary. We may double back, read again, or return to a book or article later. In these ways reading is slightly more reliable than listening to a story or having a conversation.

Another twist occurs when reading a translated text, such as the Bible. Often there is not a one-to-one equivalence between individual words in different languages. For example, the single Hebrew word *hesed* has been translated as "covenant love and faithfulness" because one English word cannot convey the entirety of its meaning in English. And a single English word, such as "love" is used to represent at least four Greek words, each of which conveys a different shade of meaning: *agapē, philia, eros, storgē*, based upon the persons involved in the relationship. A translator needs to make this clear, perhaps by adding a modifier such as "brotherly" when translating *philia*.

Given that meaning is created as we read, it becomes clear that meaning does not lie in individual words, but rather it accrues as we read words in their larger context, bringing to bear the relationship between our stored knowledge and the text itself. For this reason, we claim that the smallest unit of meaning is found at the phrase or clause level. The question, then, is how do the words in a text play with each other in the process of making meaning as we read?

All about Words and Meaning

Even though individual words require context to become meaningful, we typically turn to an alphabetized dictionary or lexicon to find insight into a particularly difficult word as we read. An alphabetized list is probably the quickest way to access an individual word, but is this the most effective way to figure out what the word contributes to a given passage? Is there another way to organize this knowledge that will return a more effective search? Let us look at the difference between words arranged in a standard alphabetized dictionary and those arranged by topical groups. The first option groups words lexically, the second groups them semantically.

Categories: Lexical and Semantic Domains

When words share a root, they often share aspects of meaning as well. This is easily seen with the most basic change between words: pluralizing a word such as "dog" to "dogs"—My *dog* went to the dog park to play with the other *dogs*. Adding an "-ing" changes our furry pet to the verb "dogging" and adding an "-ly" makes an adverb—The child was *dogging* his father's steps *doggedly*. These examples show a shift from the concrete term "dog" to the more abstract terms "dogging" and "doggedly," which play on the doglike characteristics of loyalty and persistence. In a standard dictionary these terms would be found in alphabetical order, or clustered under the term "dog." This may be called a lexical group or **lexical domain**.

Biblical Hebrew functions in a similar way, with words that cluster together because they contain the same basic three letters, known as the root. The three letters *mlk* are at the center of a cluster of words that share aspects of ruling or reigning, such as king, queen, kingdom, dominion, and so forth. The shared lexical root gives rise to a lexical domain. In a standard Hebrew lexicon, these and other related terms would be found listed under the three-letter root. The *Strong's Concordance* has given an identifying number to each Hebrew and Greek **lexeme** in the KJV of the Bible. In addition, the volume contains both a Hebrew and a Greek dictionary to describe the meaning of each word. In this case, the identifying number from the *Strong's Concordance* has been added to the diagram in diagram 1.1. While the English terms in *Strong's* are those used in the KJV, other versions sometimes use different English words to translate the same Hebrew and Greek terms. Nonetheless, the

Strong's numbers are useful for quickly identifying the specific Hebrew or Greek term that underlies the translation, making these numbers useful in other applications. Specifically, the numbers are used to identify the original language terms in both online and commercial biblical studies software and are used in other lexica as well.

This raises another question. What if more than one original language lexeme might be translated with the same English word? In this case, how do we think about other Hebrew words that also are translated as "ruling" or "reigning"? For example, Ruth 1:1 reads: "In the days when the judges *ruled,*" although the underlying Hebrew term is not from the root *mlk*. Clearly these words are not be part of the same lexical domain but are clearly associated with one another. In this case, the category would widen to become a **semantic domain**.

Diagram 1.1 *Lexical domains*

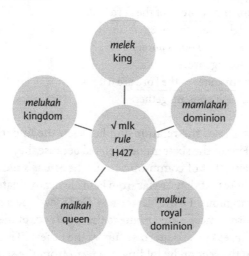

While lexical domains cluster around lexically related words, a group of words that are similar in meaning create a semantic domain. Semantic domains provide another way of categorizing words, which is extremely helpful when reading longer stretches of text. Semantic domains also play into literary features such as **metaphor** and can be used to create structure in speech and thought that finds its way to written material, including the biblical text.

Example: Psalm 19:7–9

The list in Psalm 19:7-9 contains a cluster of terms that cohere because they come from the same semantic domain. Here the psalmist has chosen a series of words from the semantic domain of communication, with one outlier—the term "fear" in verse 9 is from the semantic domain of status.

> PSALM 19:7-9 (NRSV)
>
> [7]The **law** of the Lord is perfect,
>   reviving the soul;
> the **decrees** of the Lord are sure,
>   making wise the simple;
> [8]the **precepts** of the Lord are right,
>   rejoicing the heart;
> the **commandment** of the Lord is clear,
>   enlightening the eyes;
> [9]*the fear of the Lord* is pure,
>   enduring forever;
> the **ordinances** of the Lord are true
>   and righteous altogether.

Diagram 1.2 shows the relationship between the underlined terms in Psalm 19:7-9. Five of the six terms are related because they occupy the same semantic domain, that of communication. The *Strong's* numbers included for each term show that they are far from being lexically related, as the numbers are not contiguous. Five of the terms—"God's law," "decrees," "precepts," "commands," "ordinances"—contribute to the coherence of the section, while the term "fear" breaks the pattern set up by the others. This pattern break adds interest to the section by folding in a term from the semantic domain of honor or respect.

For further discussion of semantic domains in biblical studies it is worth looking at the rise in the study of semantic domains by linguists and biblical scholars as well, including the seminal work of Johannes Louw and Eugene Nida.

Diagram 1.2 *Semantic domains*

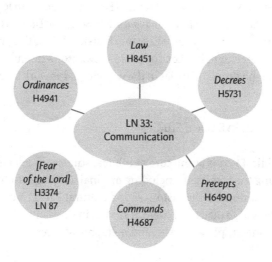

Short History

In the late 1970s and the early 1980s interest in language study shifted from analyzing and describing texts to the examination of language in use. To a large degree this was driven by the burgeoning of artificial intelligence and the rise of technology. Getting computers and humans to communicate seemed nearly impossible at first, but—Siri, anyone?—alongside the development of artificial intelligence, linguists such as Charles Fillmore and George Lakoff, and grammarians such as Ronald Langacker, began to explore language from a cognitive perspective. The claims of linguists and scholars of the "cognitive turn" include the ideas that language is integral to our entire conceptual system, that grammar is conceptualization, and that our knowledge of language comes from using language. These presuppositions have helped to form the way language is studied and viewed today and form the backbone of this volume.

In the 1980s Johannes P. Louw and Eugene A. Nida saw that there was room for improvement in the way that standard biblical studies lexica had been organized. They conceived of reorganizing the information based upon a semantic domain approach. The result, *The Greek English Lexicon of the New Testament Based on Semantic Domains*, which was first published by the United Bible Society in 1988, with a second edition in 1996. The highlight of the volume is a well-conceived list of semantic domains and sub-domains, which has proven useful not only for categorizing Biblical Greek, but for other languages as well. This was demonstrated by the work of James Swanson, who used the Louw-Nida domain numbers (LN) to keep track of myriad Hebrew lexemes. In 1997, Swanson's volume, *A Dictionary of Biblical Languages with Semantic Domains: Hebrew (Old Testament)* was published by Logos Research Systems. While this project was separate from the Greek-English Lexicon project, Swanson's careful use of the same framework highlights similarities in the way languages work across cultures.

Related Features in Biblical Studies

Since the biblical text is at the core of biblical studies, much effort goes into understanding the text itself, including original language study, literary observations, and study of the historical and cultural backgrounds of the text. Words and language matter for biblical studies in three notable ways: the role of words in context, **parallelism**, and metaphor studies.

Words in Context

Because the biblical text is a translated text for many readers, it is important to be aware of the translation theory that stands behind a given translation. Since there is no one-to-one equivalence between Hebrew or Greek as the source language and English, Dutch, German, or any possible target language, translators will work somewhere on a continuum. Some will go for the closest word-for-word translation possible, while others will opt for a dynamic-equivalence translation, one that focuses on the meaning in the target language. In English, the New American Standard Bible (NASB) would be an example of the first, and the New International Version (NIV) would be an example of the second. Duvall and Hayes (2012) provide a full analysis of many English translations. Because of these differences, on occasion there will be a variety of English words used to translate a given Hebrew or Greek word in a passage. This is where standard word studies come in—concordances, lexica, *Strong's* numbers, and other reference works.

Parallelism

Parallelism has long been recognized as a feature of Biblical Hebrew poetry. In the mid-1700s, Bishop Robert Lowth became one of the earliest English scholars to observe the role of parallelism in the Hebrew text. In Lecture 19 in his series, *Lectures on the Sacred Poetry of the Hebrews,* Lowth categorized parallel lines as *synonymous, antithetic,* or *synthetic* (neither synonymous nor antithetic). However, Lowth's handy categories are not without limitations. Often lines that are purported to be synonymous are not quite synonymous. Words are used that are close in meaning, but not precisely the same. For example, Psalm 114:5–6 (NRSV) reads:

> [5]Why is it, O sea, that you flee?
> O Jordan, that you turn back?
> [6]O mountains, that you skip like rams?
> O hills, like lambs?

The lines are satisfyingly symmetrical, but at the lexical level, the sea and the Jordan are not synonymous. Neither are the mountains and hills, nor are the rams and lambs. Similar, but not synonymous. In his volume, *The Idea of Biblical Poetry: Parallelism and Its History,* James Kugel argues that there is one form of parallelism or a hundred, not just three. His main thought is that the second line "seconds" the first, thus both reinforcing it and adding meaning. Kugel's observations regarding synonymy and its close cousin, antithesis, bear thinking about. In what ways are two lines related to one another? What causes lines to appear to be synonymous or antithetical? What do we gain by categorizing lines in this way? Adele Berlin examines these questions from a linguistic perspective in her volume *The Dynamics of Biblical Parallelism,* offering several angles on how linguistic features create parallel lines or thoughts. She adds the idea of "distant parallelism" to the discussion, noting that the first and last lines of a section can be related in a way that sandwiches the entire section together. While lexical issues such as words and phrases play a part, Berlin also considers grammatical, semantic, structural, phonetic, and psychological aspects as well, noting how they all interact in forming parallel thoughts.

Metaphor

Metaphor and **simile** are two prevalent literary features that create interest when reading a text. The Bible is full of metaphor, simile, and other literary features. Simile is clearly present in Psalm 114, with mountains and hills that are skipping "like" rams and lambs. However, there is no "like" or "as" present regarding the fleeing sea and the turning Jordan. By directly addressing these bodies of water, the psalmist has personalized them, giving them character-istics of sentient beings: they are spoken to as if they are expected to hear and respond. They appear to have made a choice to flee and to turn back. These phrases contain aspects of both literary and conceptual metaphor. The psalmist has used characteristics of humankind to understand characteristics of creation.

Words and Meaning in Biblical Studies

Context is everything in biblical studies. Being aware of the text on the page seems at times to be the main goal. Because the Bible is translated text, we spend a lot of time seeking out the most accurate meaning for words and phrases. We look for the way that the words function in the text, in surround-ing texts of similar genre, in works by the same author and those of different authors. We look for information from history and archaeology to fill in our understandings of the ancient situation, all good and necessary approaches.

However, one of the first tasks of reading well is to interpret the interpreter, which is often considered a secondary activity. Importantly, as readers, we bring great quantities of encyclopedic background knowledge of the world to the text and nothing says "aware reader" more than understanding our own often cul-turally shaped preunderstandings and presuppositions. Preunderstandings are those things we take for granted—our innate views of gender, cultural markers, and so on. Our presuppositions may be more reflective and thought-out and at times shaped by our reading community: is the Bible inspired, infallible, our rule of faith and practice, great literature, or a cultural artifact? Where we start will often determine how we read. This includes our view of translation and the importance of dealing well with languages not our own.

The Role of Language in Structure and Literariness

The biblical text is filled with structural details such as parallelism and with literary features such as metaphor and metonymy. The effectiveness of both parallelism and literary features owes a lot to the lexical choices of the author. By looking at these choices in light of semantic domains, several things be-come clear. First, because there are no true synonyms, parallel lines may or may not depend strictly on word pairs in order to be perceived as synonymous or antithetical parallelism (or a combination of the two in longer groups of verses). While some think these ancient categories are not sufficient, clearly similarity and oppositeness are present in many sets of parallel lines. Recategorizing the key terms and phrases as members of the same semantic domain makes it possible to see where the lines cohere or diverge. Since the semantic domain provides a principled category for terms from many lexical domains, it can act as an overarching category.

Likewise, literary metaphor—that pervasive literary feature that makes a comparison without the use of "like" or "as"—depends heavily on the choice of lexemes from varying semantic domains. In this case, the semantic domains are often quite different from one another. In fact, the more different, the more vivid the metaphor may become. Often metaphor moves between entities that are on different levels of an animacy hierarchy, for example, comparing a human being to an animal. Psalm 22:16a, b (NRSV) reads: "For dogs are all around me; a company of evildoers encircles me." In these sentences, the term "dogs" and the phrase "a company of evildoers" seem to be related but are not from the same lexical or semantic domains. In this case, the terms are quite far from one another in the meaning department. Underlying the metaphor is an easily recognizable conceptual metaphor, A HUMAN IS AN ANIMAL. The metaphor makes a comparison between an animal and a human, and a rather unfavorable comparison at that—clearly the company of evildoers bear some resemblance to ravening dogs, a disturbing image indeed.

Case Study: Semantic Domains in the Language of Psalm 119

Psalm 119, known as the longest psalm, is a unique literary creation that demonstrates a keen sense of organization at the textual level and also exhibits a remarkable degree of cohesion due to the artistic use of a repeated group of terms chosen from the LN 33, the semantic domain of communication. The psalm is an alphabetic acrostic. Unlike other alphabetic acrostics where each individual line starts with successive letters of the Hebrew alphabet, Psalm 119 is divided into eight-line sections and all lines in a given section begin with the same letter of the Hebrew alphabet. This example will look at the first two sections, *Aleph* (vv. 1–8) and *Bet* (vv. 9–16).

Psalm 119 contains a rich selection of terms from the semantic domain of communication, as laid out in table 1.1: semantic domains in Psalm 119. This feature complements the nature of the psalm as a communication event, complete with a speaker, a hearer, and a message. Interestingly, for the first three verses the communication event focuses on the psalmist and the reader. At verse 4, the focus shifts to a communication event between the psalmist and God, as marked by the second person terms "you" and "your" that pepper the remainder of the psalm.

Each of the communication terms occur in phrases, rather than as individual terms. The psalmist addresses God in a personal way, speaking about "*your* statutes, *your* decrees, *your* commandments" and so forth. The second person term "your" adds specificity to the communication terms—these are not generic statutes, decrees, and commandments, but come from God himself. The *Strong's* numbers attached to the terms indicate that the terms come from different lexical domains, while the LN numbers indicate they are from the same semantic domain, with some shared subdomains that indicate different types of communication events.

It is tempting to look for parallelism in the lines of Psalm 119. After all, the psalm is carefully structured into eight-line sections, so lower-level correlations seem likely as well. Psalm 119:1a–2b (NRSV) looks like a likely match:

> ¹Happy are those whose way is blameless,
>   who walk in the **law** of the Lord.
> ²Happy are those who keep his **decrees**,
>   who seek him with their whole heart.

At first glance, the exactly synonymous phrase "Happy are those" appears to indicate synonymous parallelism. However, in this regard, it is helpful to note that the following pairs of phrases are similar but not identical, either grammatically or semantically. The phrase "whose way is blameless" in verse 1a correlates best with the phrase "who seek him with their whole heart" in verse 2b. Both describe upright humans, but not in precisely the same way. Likewise, the phrase "who walk in the **law** of the Lord" in verse 1b seems to correlate best with the phrase "who keep his **decrees**" in verse 2a. Structurally, there is a low-level chiasm here that adds interest. However, the semantic difference between "law" and "decrees" begs the question of how alike the two actions or attitudes are. As table 1.1 suggests, the two terms come from two LN subdomains, "law" from 33.35 and "decrees" from 33.262–33.273. A deep dive into the subdomains is not necessary to see that while both are from the domain of communication, they are not completely synonymous. So, while the lines are similar enough to be deemed a parallelism, they are not identical either grammatically or semantically.

In Psalm 119:9–16 the English term "word" appears in both verse 9 and verse 16. Each of these verses ends with the phrase "your word." This creates a distant parallelism or *inclusio* that frames the section. Verse 11 also contains the English phrase, "your word," but in this case, it is from a different root. They are semantically related, and the use of the two terms creates interest in the Hebrew text. It is also good to note that while the first term is often construed as written or codified communication, the second refers to oral communication in most instances. It is the Hebrew equivalent of the "he said, she said" verb of speaking in English.

Table 1.1 *Semantic domains in Psalm 119*

Transliteration	English	Lexical Domains *Strong's #*	Semantic Domain LN 33 communication	Ps 119:1–8	Ps 119:9–16
torah	law	H8451	LN 33.35	v. 1	
dabar	word	H1697	LN 33.69–33.108		vv. 9, 16
edot	decrees	H5713	LN 33.262–33.273	v. 2	v. 14
piqqudim	precepts	H6490	LN 33.333–33.342	vv. 4	v. 15
huqqim	statutes	H2706	LN 33.333–33.342	vv. 5, 8	vv. 12, 16
mitzvot	commandments	H4687	LN 33.323–33.332	v. 6	v. 10
mishpatim	ordinances	H4941	LN 33.333–33.342	v. 7	v. 13
imrah	saying, word	H565	LN 33.69–33.108		v. 11

Cruising on through the remaining communication terms in these sections, it becomes apparent that a net of meaning is created because of the use of the group of terms that share the same semantic domain, LN 33: communication. The accrued meaning is greater than the sum of the parts and the psalmist is quite persuasive in his admiration for all forms of God's communication.

PSALM 119:1–8 (NRSV)

¹Happy are those whose way is blameless,
    who walk in the **law** of the Lord.
²Happy are those who keep his **decrees**,
    who seek him with their whole heart,

³who also do no wrong,
　　but walk in his **ways**.
⁴You have commanded your **precepts**
　　to be kept diligently.
⁵O that my ways may be steadfast
　　in keeping your **statutes**!
⁶Then I shall not be put to shame,
　　having my eyes fixed on all your **commandments**.
⁷I will praise you with an upright heart,
　　when I learn your righteous **ordinances**.
⁸I will observe your **statutes**;
　　do not utterly forsake me.

PSALM 119:9–16 (NRSV)

⁹How can young people keep their way pure?
　　By guarding it according to your **word**.
¹⁰With my whole heart I seek you;
　　do not let me stray from your **commandments**.
¹¹I treasure your **word** in my heart,
　　so that I may not sin against you.
¹²Blessed are you, O LORD;
　　teach me your **statutes**.
¹³With my lips I declare
　　all the **ordinances** of your mouth.
¹⁴I delight in the way of your **decrees**
　　as much as in all riches.
¹⁵I will meditate on your **precepts**,
　　and fix my eyes on your **ways**.
¹⁶I will delight in your **statutes**;
　　I will not forget your **word**.

Ideas for Discussion

1. Choose another eight-line section from Psalm 119. Using the information in table 1.1, see how many of the terms appear in your section. Make some observations about how the terms are used. For example, look at syntax: Do the terms appear at the beginning or end of the sentence? Look more closely at how the

semantic domain is deployed across the verses: Are there repeated terms? Are there terms in the sequence that come from different semantic domains? Look at the contrasts present between the words in the communication domain and the comparisons being made by the psalmist. How do the overlaying meanings of the terms color the psalmist's message?

2. Read the following passages and note the way the psalmist talks about God.

   - 2 Samuel 22:2
   - Psalm 18:2
   - Psalm 71:3
   - Psalm 91:1
   - Psalm 144:2

Address the following questions: What terms does the psalmist use to describe his relationship to God? Is there a common idea that underlies each of the comparisons? How might the psalmist's conceptualization of his relationship with God bring comfort? Assurance? Can you think of ways that these metaphors reflect the ancient Near Eastern context in which the psalmist lived?

3. Psalm 115:2–8 draws a comparison between "Our God" and the gods of the nations. Read the following verses, noting the words and phrases in verses 5–7 that the psalmist uses to describe the idols of the nations, all of which come from the semantic domain LN 8: body parts. What is the tone of the section? What is the poetic effect of this series of sentences?

> [2] Why should the nations say,
> "Where is their God?"
> [3] Our God is in the heavens;
> he does whatever he pleases.
> [4] Their idols are silver and gold,
> the work of human hands.
> [5] They have mouths, but do not speak;
> eyes, but do not see.
> [6] They have ears, but do not hear;
> noses, but do not smell.
> [7] They have hands, but do not feel;
> feet, but do not walk;
> they make no sound in their throats.
> [8] Those who make them are like them;
> so are all who trust in them. (NRSV)

THE BITS AND PIECES OF READING

Further Reading

Working with words is a well-discussed area in biblical studies. A few resources stand out, including the clearly written method for doing a word study from the English text in J. Scott Duvall and J. Daniel Hays, *Grasping God's Word: A Hands-on Approach to Reading, Interpreting, and Applying the Bible* (2012). This is an ideal starting point for learning established methods. The intrepid will enjoy a foray into Johannes P. Louw and Eugene Albert Nida, *Greek-English Lexicon of the New Testament: Based on Semantic Domains* (1996). This volume contains the rationale behind using semantic domain for categorizing Greek terms. The Hebrew companion volume is James Swanson, *Dictionary of Biblical Languages with Semantic Domains: Hebrew (Old Testament)* (1997).

TWO

Building Categories

The Use of Prototypes

About Model Children

Children occasionally appear in the Bible. Think of the birth account of Cain and Abel in Genesis 4, Jephthah's daughter in Judges 11-12, or the babies in Solomon's judgment in 1 Kings 3. *The* child of the book of Genesis, and perhaps the entire Old Testament, is Isaac, beloved and only son, almost sacrificed to God by his father Abraham. Equally beloved, but in the New Testament, is the child Jesus. The evangelists recount stories featuring a baby or young boy Jesus, such as his birth account in Matthew 1-2 and Luke 2 as well as his dedication to the temple in Luke 2. When Jesus dies, as an adult, his address to his heavenly Father reminds us that he is, despite his age, still the child of his parent.

All about Prototypes

When readers come across each of these children in the Bible, they will try to categorize them. Are Cain and Abel children? And what about Isaac or Jesus? Is there a moment when they stop being children? This identification of characters as members of a particular group is a crucial aspect of reading. When people read, they categorize. They wonder to which group something or someone belongs. What is more, they not only figure out whether, for example, Isaac is a child, but also how much of a child he is. In order to answer that question, readers compare Isaac with their *best example* of a child, called a **prototype**. This prototype forms the basis of their classification and functions as a reference point to categorize other children. The distance or proximity to this prototypical child will deter-mine how well Isaac fits the category of children. A prototype is a men-tal picture, based on all the children one has met, read about, and heard about in life. It is not a fixed image, but one that undergoes refinement and changes over time.

Diagram 2.1 *Category child with prototype*

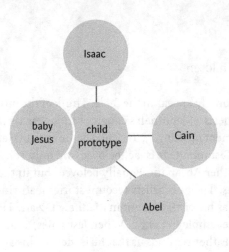

Prototypes come with *attributes*, that is, identifying characteristics. For a child, such would be underage, naïve, little to no responsibility, someone in need of a guardian, not self-providing, loves to play, and so on. Say one reads the story of the prodigal son in Luke 15. Is this son a child? He surely is naïve and not capable of providing for himself. However, he also seems to be of age and at least initially independent enough to live on his own. Readers may categorize the prodigal son as a child, but not as the best one. The son is not a *central* example of their child category, but at the same time he is not that far remote from the child prototype that he becomes entirely peripheral. Note that such is not a problem for categories defined by prototypes. They do not require members to share all the features of the best example of the category, but rather define membership in terms of degree. As a result, a reader can still consider the prodigal son to be a child, even when he does not share certain attributes with the prototype of the category.

Diagram 2.2 *Radial structure of category child with prodigal son*

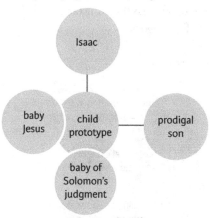

To visualize prototypicality, scholars use a **radial structure**, as presented in diagram 2.2. In the center, the best example of the category, the prototype, is found. Around it, all other manifestations of the category are placed. Close resemblance to the prototype results in a position very near to the center. Slight resemblance leads to a position at the outskirts of the radial structure. The boundaries of a category are fuzzy, meaning that it is unclear where a category ends and a new one begins. Is the prodigal son a child, because he is naïve and needs his father's protection, or is he an adult, because he leaves the house to live on his own?

Diagram 2.3 *Fuzzy boundaries*

In general, people have a good sense of basic level categories, such as "child," this in contrast to broader categories, such as family, or more specific categories, such as a one-year-old child. When asked to draw a basic level category, people will easily do so, whereas the same task would be deemed more difficult for general and specific categories.

Diagram 2.4 *Basic level categories*

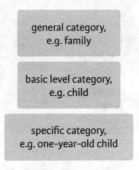

Up until now, we have applied prototypes and categories to characters in a story. Yet, categorization happens for various other elements of the text as well, and this from the level of words over that of Bible books to the entire Bible. What is more, categories can refer to story elements, such as characters, but also to linguistic structures that help to build the story, such as **parallelism**. Let us consider some examples to clarify this.

Example 1: A Structural Category on Micro-Level

One of the identifying features of biblical poetry is its use of parallelism. Parallelism is a repetition of the structure or content of a line in the next line of the text. The opening of Psalm 93, for example, reads:[1]

(1) The LORD	(he) reigns
(2) with height	he is dressed,
(3) (he) is dressed	the LORD,
(4) with strength	he is girded.
(5) (It) stands firm	the world,
(6) it will not totter.	

1. All translations are the author's own.

Lines 2 and 4 are parallel in structure. They both have a nonverbal part followed by a verb: "with height" / "with strength" – "he is dressed" / "he is girded." What is more, they are also parallel in content, expressing the same idea with different words. "Height" and "strength" function as synonyms, as do "dressing" and "girding." Lines 5 and 6 are parallel in content but not in structure. If the world "stands firm," it means it will indeed "not totter." Lines 1 and 3 are not parallel, at first sight. Whereas the dress can be considered a signal of God's kingship, and thus a parallel in content to some degree, such is not true for the structure. Lines 1 and 3 have a different order of subject and verb: "the LORD" / "he is dressed" – "(he) reigns" / "the LORD."

Diagram 2.5 *Radial structure of category parallelism*

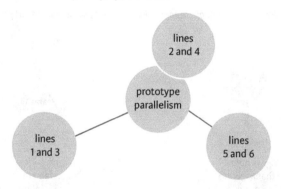

In order to distinguish parallel lines from nonparallel lines and determine the degree of parallelism, readers compare the verses of the psalm with their prototype of parallelism. This prototype will tell you that the parallelism between lines 2 and 4 is a strong example, with a parallelism in both content and structure. Yet also the other examples will be categorized as parallelism, although further away from the center of the radial structure. As readers go through more biblical poetry, they will adapt their idea of what the best example of a parallelism is. They will see that parallelism comes in various forms, some examples clearly parallel, others sort of parallel or even vaguely parallel. Otherwise put, some lines are more parallel than others.

Example 2: A Category on Mid-Level

Mid-level categories focus on the categorization of (larger) parts of the Bible, for example, the category of thanksgiving psalms or laments. Psalm 23 comes close to the central example of that category: "The LORD is my shepherd; I shall not want." The speaker is praising God's protection and love. In comparison, Psalm 13 presents a speaker who feels abandoned and lonely: "How long, LORD, will you forget me forever?" In the closing lines of Psalm 13, however, the psalmist expresses his trust in God and sings his praise: "I will sing to the LORD, because he has been good to me." Thus, Psalm 13 belongs to at least two categories of psalms, although overall it may be a better example of lament than of thanksgiving.

Diagram 2.6 *Radial structure of category thanksgiving psalm and lament psalm*

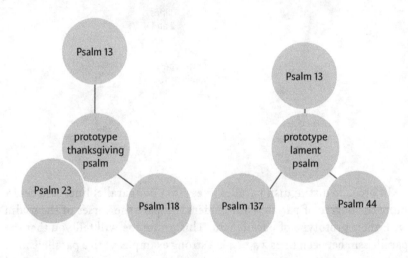

Example 3: A Category on Macro-Level

A nice example of prototypes and the entire Bible is the question of whether the Bible is literature. When faced with this question, readers will compare the features of the biblical text with the literary prototype in their mind. Below is an example of a possible radial structure of the category "literature" including the Bible.

Diagram 2.7 *Radial structure of category literature*

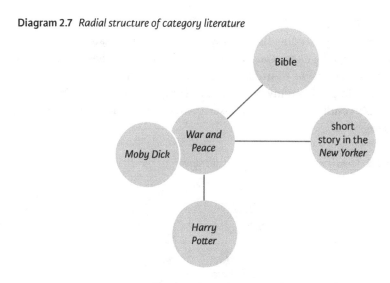

In this categorization, *War and Peace* by Leo Tolstoy functions as a proto-typical example of the category "literature." It tells a fictional story in a stylized manner, presenting well-developed characters whose adventures and emotions form the focus of the book. These are a few attributes of this specific literary prototype. Another good example is *Moby Dick*, whereas *Harry Potter* and a short story in *The New Yorker* appear as poorer examples. A reader may, for example, consider the *Harry Potter* series too popular to be literature, and a short story too short to present well-developed characters. If we now try to position the Bible in relation to this prototype, we can say that it presents a story of God and his people, written in a particular style, but that we would not deem it "fictional" nor particularly interested in characters' emotions beyond their relationship with God. Therefore, the Bible would be considered a member of the category, but neither the best example nor the worst.

The presented radial structure, above, is a possible categorization. Prototypes are dynamic and so is the process of categorization that makes use of them. This flexibility is inherent to the fact that prototypes are based on experiences. Scholars therefore say that prototypes are embodied, that is, the fact that we experience the world with and through our bodies affects our categories. Thus, prototypes are not fixed images without context, but evolve as we go through new experiences. To return to the example of the Bible as literature, imagine I have read books such as *The Secret History* (Donna Tartt), *De ontdekking van de hemel* (Harry Mulish), *The Odyssey* (Homer), and *Matilda* (Roald Dahl). In addition, I have seen movies based on some of these books, such as *Matilda* (1996) and *The Discovery of Heaven* (2001). Some of the books were on my college reading lists. In my second year, for example, I worked my way through the entire *Odyssey* in classical Greek. All these experiences influence my prototype of literature. My personal experiences render my prototype different from my neighbor's or from, say, a Peruvian farmer in his 50s. As a result, our individual assessments of the Bible as literature will vary as well.

Diagram 2.8 *Radial structure of my category literature*

Diagram 2.9 *Radial structure of category literature of Peruvian farmer*

Perhaps even more important than individual experience is the *sociocultural setting* for categorization. Whereas my neighbor and I share a common background as far as the time and place we live in, the Peruvian male mentioned above lives in different sociocultural circumstances. Context determines to a high degree the basic setup of prototypes. Education, cultural background, and even national identity, they all play into our prototypes. I, as a European woman with an academic background in classics and ancient Near Eastern studies, consider the Bible literature. My literary prototype is influenced by the way I was brought up (with lots of books in the house), my education (with more books to read), and all the books I have read in various languages (which is partially explained by the fact that I live in a trilingual country and my mother tongue, Dutch, is not a world language). The Bible is not my most central example of the category "literature," but it is close enough for it to be identified as such.

Diagram 2.10 *Influences of prototype construal*

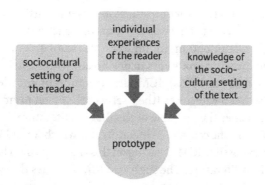

However, imagine the Peruvian male in his 50s is a farmer. He knows his Bible, in Spanish, as well as a few classics in Spanish, which he may or may not have read himself. These works determine his literary prototype. Most likely he will not categorize the Bible as literature, or maybe only as a peripheral example. Because in his mindset, the Bible is God's word and all those literary works are the product of people. They talk about other, less important things, whereas the Bible speaks about God.

Short History

The notion of prototypes stems from *cognitive psychology*. In her studies on color, Eleanor Rosch (1973a) discovered that people categorize colors proto-

THE BITS AND PIECES OF READING

typically, with best examples and poorer examples of the same color. People consider some variants of, for example, red to be "redder" than others. The best examples of the category are the so-called focal colors, and this regardless of how many color terms a language has. In other words, categories are as much the result of the mind as of bodily experience. This is precisely what we have illustrated above, with the categorization of the prodigal son as a child or the Bible as literature. Categories are not just book definitions, but draw on what we have seen, read, and experienced ourselves as well.

Further studies with other items, such as fruit or vehicles, revealed the same tendencies found in the color studies (Rosch 1975; Rosch and Mervis 1975). Again, participants consistently classified certain examples as better than others, in a graded manner rather than based on an in-or-out distinction. *Cognitive linguists* applied the theory to study various aspects of language, for example, semantic issues such as **polysemy** (Do polysemous words have a central meaning with the other meanings as closer or further away from it?) and **markedness** (What can we learn from constructions that deviate from the unmarked, default option, in, for example, word order of a sentence?). Linguists often mention prototypes in one breath with **Idealized Cognitive Models** (abbreviated as **ICMs**). ICMs are structures of knowledge that rely on relations between categories (themselves relying on prototypes). As an illustration, consider the example of the Bible as literature. We considered whether the Bible fit the category of literature, for which we had *War and Peace* as a prototype. A possible ICM, drawing on this category, could be a discussion about the Bible as literature. The suggested ICM includes the typical participants in a discussion, turn-taking, how you build an argument, etc. ICMs, just like prototypes, are generalizations that are the result of multiple experiences with, in this case, literary texts. Examples of ICMs will be discussed more fully in part 2 (Mapping Corresponding Dots).

Related Features in Biblical Studies

There are at least three areas in which the idea of categorization and prototypes is (mostly) implicitly present in biblical studies: discussions on genre, modality, and intertextuality. **Genre** is a subject that has interested biblical scholars from the beginning. What kind of text is the biblical text taken as a whole, and what about its parts? Scholars have addressed the genre question from different angles, most notably as a combination of literary patterns and their history. Thus, they (re)constructed a list of features for each genre as well

32

as the actual setting from which these genres originated. For example, some psalms were thought of as having a cultic context. One group of researchers, those of apocalyptic texts, interprets categorization more along the lines of the prototypes discussed in this chapter. They consider genres to be subjective constructs with an internal coherence. In other words, an apocalyptic text is not identified by ticking off a list of required features that determines whether it is in or out of the category. Instead, one distinguishes the apocalyptic genre by looking at the overall appearance of a text or passage of text to consequently consider how close or far away this is from the apocalyptic prototype.

Another area in which prototypes underlie the discussion is that of the **modality** of the biblical text. Oral, written, or performed, how should we classify the text? And what does such a classification mean for our overall understanding of the Bible? Historical, anthropological, and linguistic research has shown that the biblical text, even though we only have a written document left, includes features of different modes without being necessarily only one or the other. In terms of prototypes, one could say that some passages in the text are better examples of oral language whereas other passages are better examples of written language or performative language.

Third, prototypes are tacitly used when studying **intertextuality**. Intertextuality looks at the relationship between different texts. For example, did a text copy a fragment of another one? Is it a quote or a rephrasing? And if it is the latter, how close is the rephrasing to the original? In other words, taking the original text as the prototype, scholars compare other texts and fragments of text to figure out the relationship between the prototype and the other text. For example, how do readers classify the "new heaven and earth" of Third Isaiah and the creation narrative in Genesis 1? And what do they do with a biblical passage and a passage from a nonbiblical text, such as the Babylonian flood narrative or Milton's *Paradise Lost*?

The Meaning of Prototypes in Biblical Studies

As the above overview shows, prototypes touch upon some of the key questions that have driven biblical scholarship. Deciding about the genre of the Bible, the genre of a specific text, or the relation between texts is part of the reading process. Prototypes help us understand how these decisions are made and what influences them. More specifically, prototypicality teaches us about the flexibility and fluidity of categories. If the Bible is classified as literature, it does not mean that it can no longer be identified as a document of faith. King

David can still fit our category of leader, even when he sleeps with Bathsheba or sends her husband to a sudden death.

Prototypes come in particularly handy for the study of all those passages and issues that are considered problematic. There are many texts that do not fit the category assigned to them. There are plenty of stories where heroes do unheroic things. Prototypes are a tool to reassess categories, and this at various levels. For example, on a micro-level, one can think of categories, such as the hero, the divine, or gender. When readers come across the story of Samson in Judges, how would they classify him? Is he a hero? Where would he be positioned in our radial structure of the category "hero"? In order to understand a reading of Samson as character, one should also consider the prototypes of the reader's world. Obviously, the twenty-first-century western idea of a hero is different from that of the patriarchal society in which the story is set. How does the hero prototype of the reader affect the categorization of Samson? And ultimately, how does it influence the reading and understanding of the Samson narrative?

As an example of a mid-level categorization, the genre of the book of Jonah forms a good case study. It carries various labels: comedy, parody, fiction, parable. The list of labels already suggests that the Jonah text may benefit from a prototypical approach. It makes more sense to call the text "kind of a parody" and "slightly fictional." This formulation indicates two things: (1) that the Jonah text belongs to at least two categories, that of parody and that of fiction; and (2) that it is for neither category the best example, thus the prototype, but nevertheless a member of that category. Again, the categorization of the Jonah text can be set against the sociocultural context of the reader. What is fiction in an ancient setting? And what does the category look like today? Similarly, would a South-Korean reader of Jonah consider Jonah fiction? And if so, would the radial structure of that category be similar to that of a French reader or an American one?

In the end, prototypes will allow us to reassess the categorization of the Bible as a text. How much of a document of faith is it? And what about its degree of literariness, fictionality, and historicity? This categorization will both explore the Bible's position within each of the suggested categories as well as the fuzziness of the boundaries between them.

Similar to the notion of figure and ground, prototypes are so fundamental to human language and thinking that they can be considered in various studies, from the prototype of the patriarch (a sociohistorical study) or that of the city (an urban studies topic) to the prototype of divine speech (a theolinguistic study) or that of evil (an ethical question). As the above examples show, prototypes and categories help us to understand both the world of the biblical text and our interpretation of that world which is influenced by the sociocultural setting in which we read the text. Prototypes show us where the various readings of the biblical text come from. At the same time, they demonstrate that these interpretations are guided by various, although not unlimited, factors.

Case Study: The Birth of Jesus

As a case study, let us look at the birth narrative of Jesus in Matthew, and not at baby Jesus, but at the *Magi* or wise men in this story. In Matthew 2, Herod hears about Jesus's birth through wise men who can read the stars. These characters are known in the Christian tradition as the kings that bring their gifts to Jesus. According to this tradition (not the text itself), one of them is identified as dark (from the twentieth century onward, explicitly black). The religious and cultural reception of the text suggests that these people, consulted and sent by Herod, are prototypical strangers. But how does the text categorize them?

> [1] After Jesus was born in Bethlehem in Judea, during the time of King Herod, *Magi from the east* came to Jerusalem [2] and asked, "Where is the one who has been born king of the Jews? We saw his *star* when it rose and have come to worship him."...
>
> [7] Then Herod called the *Magi secretly* and found out from them the *exact time the star had appeared.* [8] He *sent them* to Bethlehem and said, "Go and search carefully for the child. As soon as you find him, report to me, so that I too may go and worship him."... [11] Then they opened their *treasures* and presented him with *gifts of gold, frankincense and myrrh.* [12] And having been *warned in a dream* not to go back to Herod, they *returned to their country* by another route.
>
> ... [16] When Herod learned that he had been *outwitted by the Magi* ...

The wise men are introduced in verse 1 as coming from the east to Jerusalem. Hence, they are not part of Joseph and Mary's people nor are they members of Herod's people. This is made explicit through the mentioning of their return to their own land in verse 12. They are foreigners. Not only their origin but also their customs play into their categorization as strangers. They can read the stars and understand dreams. Such is at odds with the practices of the visited country, as the secret meeting with Herod suggests. In addition, they carry exotic gifts with them, another sign of their outlandishness. Finally, the foreigners are not only described with a sort of admiration but also as a sort of enemies, who eventually betray Herod. They do not report back to the king as he had asked. The wise men in the text come very close to a prototype of foreigner: different country of residence and origin, different customs, different commodities, and no loyalty to the leader of the country they visit.

However, the Magi can also be identified as some sort of tourists: they come for a visit and return to their country. Note again the formulation here: the wise men can be placed somewhere on the graded continuum of the category of "tourist." Where exactly depends on a reader's own prototype of tourist. A few attributes seem to be present: the aspect of temporary travel with the same starting and end point, the intention to see something (the star and the child), and the liberty to not obey the king of the visited country.

Finally, the text also suggests that the Magi are a type of learned men, with astrological and magical knowledge. The very word that names them denotes a class of Zoroastrian priests from Parthia. The East, mentioned in the text, is typically the place where such knowledge was present. Think of the Babylonian astronomers for the Old Testament and the Chinese Tao for the western tradition. Wisdom traditionally comes from the East. The fact that Herod meets them secretly adds to their powerful but at the same time perhaps forbidden, or at least shady, skills. These skills, in the form of dream interpretation, make them go back home instead of to Herod. The result is described as deception; they are tricksters.

The above analysis illustrates how the Magi in this birth narrative of Jesus can belong to at least three different categories of which the boundaries are fuzzy. The text offers elements that support an argumentation for a membership to each of them. The eventual categorization of the reader depends on which cues they decide to follow. Such is influenced by the reader's previous experiences with foreigners, tourists, and wise men, respectively. The sociocultural context plays an important role as well. Nowadays, tourism is far more popularized and comes with selfies and social media. The wise men today would either be scientists (without the magic) or spiritual figures, each with their own attributes. Finally, one should not underestimate the impact of the view of the Magi that is passed on in families to children (think of the nativity set with three kings with distinct colors) and that forms a reference point for their later readings: Gaspar, Melchior, and Balthasar are already categorized before most people read the story by Matthew. For the record, Matthew's story does not mention skin color, names, or even the number of wise men. The categorization of the Magi plays a role in the broader interpretation of the birth narrative. It is a basic level process which the given analysis makes explicit.

Ideas for Discussion

1. Read the story of Jael and Sisera in Judges 4 and 5 in which different gender roles are very prominent. How does the text construe the prototype of male and female gender? What is the role of the sociocultural setting of the biblical text in this construction? And how does the setting of a modern-day reader influence the categorization and interpretation of gender in the story?

2. The book of Judges features several leaders, called judges. Where would you position each of the judges mentioned in the book? Which judge do you consider the best example and which one a poorer example of the category?

3. If you go back to your categorization of judges, which of the stories do you remember best? If told to mention one story, which one would you name? In other words, do you see a relationship between the prototypicality of a story or a character and its effect on the reader?

4. Can you think of other characters, events, or stories in the Bible that have a great impact on the reader? Can you consequently think of their position within a given category, and consider whether both are related or not?

5. The Bible contains several types of texts. How would you categorize, and thus apply the notion of prototypes to the following texts? Which text is, according to you, more biblical, and which one less?

   - The prophecy of Isaiah
   - The Gospel of John
   - The Song of Songs
   - The patriarchal narratives in Genesis
   - The Letter to the Hebrews
   - The book of Lamentations
   - The book of Revelation
   - The book of Judith

6. Compare your categorization of the above texts with that of your friend, class group, family. Can you explain the differences? Think of the previously discussed individual and sociocultural elements that influence our construal of prototypes and how we categorize things.

7. The Bible can not only be categorized against other prototypes, but it has also become a prototype itself. The reception history of the Bible is long and rich. Where would you place the following works in the radial structure of the category Bible: the King James Version of the Bible, the humorous podcast *Sean and Eliot Read the Bible*, the movie *Exodus: Gods and Kings* (2014), and an illustrated children's Bible?

Further Reading

Introductions to prototypes in language and literature can be found in George Lakoff, *Women, Fire and Dangerous Things: What Categories Reveal about the Mind* (1987); John R. Taylor, *Linguistic Categorization: Prototypes in Linguistic Theory* (1995); and Peter Stockwell, *Cognitive Poetics: An Introduction* (2002, 27–40).

In the above-mentioned *Women, Fire and Dangerous Things* (1987), Lakoff gives an excellent overview of prototype theory and its history (12–57). Especially the work by Eleanor Rosch has been fundamental to the development and visibility of the theory. See, among others, Eleanor Rosch, "Natural Categories" (1973a); "On the Internal Structure of Perceptual and Semantic Categories" (1973b); "Cognitive Representations of Semantic Categories" (1975); and Rosch and Carolyn Mervis, "Family Resemblances: Studies in the Structure of Categories" (1975).

For studies on prototypes and genre, consult John Swales, *Genre Analysis: English in Academic and Research Settings* (1990); Brian Paltridge, "Working with Genre: A Pragmatic Perspective" (1995); and Michael Sinding, "After Definitions: Genre, Categories and Cognitive Science" (2002). Groundbreaking research on the Bible and genre has been conducted by Hermann Gunkel in his book *The Psalms: A Form-Critical Introduction* ([1926] 1967) and by Vincent Taylor on the synoptic gospel tradition in the work *The Formation of the Gospel Tradition: Eight Lectures* (1933). Carol Newsom points at the similarities between the approach adopted in the Semeia 14 issue *Apocalypse: The Morphology of a Genre* (1979) and prototype theory in her piece "Spying out the Land: A Report from Genology" (2007).

The modes of the biblical texts are discussed by Susan Niditch in *Oral World and Written World: Ancient Israelite Literature* (1996) and David Carr, "Introduction: The Oral-Written Model and the Formation of the Hebrew Bible" (2011). Readers can find a brief summary of research on this topic in Frank Polak, "Book, Scribe, and Bard" (2011). For a discussion regarding the New

Testament, see Larry Hurtado, "Oral Fixation and New Testament Studies? 'Orality,' 'Performance' and Reading Texts in Early Christianity" (2014).

Examples of intertextuality studies are the following: Stanley Porter, *Hearing the Old Testament in the New Testament* (2006); Richard B. Hays, Stefan Alkier, and Leroy A. Huizenga, *Reading the Bible Intertextually* (2009); Geoffrey Miller, "Intertextuality in Old Testament Research" (2011); and Niall McKay, "Status Update: The Many Faces of Intertextuality in New Testament Study" (2013).

To conclude, the following pieces discuss the role of the Magi in Jesus's birth account: Warren Carter, *Matthew and the Margins: A Socio-Political Reading and Religious Reading* (2000, 73–83); Brent Landau, *Revelation of the Magi: The Lost Tale of the Wise Men's Journey to Bethlehem* (2010); and Ian Boxall, *Matthew through the Centuries* (2019, 54–64).

THREE

Attention and Focus

Playing with Figure and Ground

Figuring It Out

Reading the book of Jonah is a journey from one place to another and from one character to another. God commands Jonah to go to Nineveh and prophesy, but Jonah turns away from that order and embarks on his own journey, away from Nineveh and away from God, with the reader on his tail. When Jonah speaks in chapter 2, his words are psalm-like, standing out against the surrounding narrative. At the end of chapter 2, the prophet realizes that he must face God and eventually in chapter 3 he fulfills his role as a prophet after all. Most peculiarly, his prophecy consists of a single line with a double meaning: "Forty more days and Nineveh shall be overthrown/overthrow itself!" (Jonah 3:4).[1] Can a vision be more compelling than that? Chapter 3 seems to resolve the remaining narrative tension when Nineveh is humbled, but in chapter 4 Jonah reenters the spotlight, questioning God's position toward the city and connecting his own fate to it.

All about Figure and Ground

Each of the above observations plays upon the concepts of figure and ground. **Figure** and **ground** are two concepts that describe the position of an object (figure) against its surroundings (ground). Typically, the figure is what draws our attention, whereas the ground is mostly neglected. Figure and ground are mobile categories, meaning that we can shift our attention, or it can be directed to a shift, so that another item becomes the figure and the original

---

1. Translations in this chapter are the author's own.

figure disappears in the background. Visually, the concepts are illustrated with images as the one below. Viewers can focus on the fruit or on the face. They can also shift from one image to the other, switching the positions of figure and ground between fruit and face.

Diagram 3.1 *Face-fruit image*

Similarly, the book of Jonah opens with God and his prophecy as figure— Jonah is only ground at that point. He is there but the narrator draws our attention to what God has to say. Our gaze shifts to Jonah when he does not follow God's command. Where is he going? What is he doing? We, as readers, are no longer with God and what will happen to Nineveh, but with Jonah's adventures on the ship and in the fish. Jonah has become the figure; Nineveh and God now form the ground. The initial positions of figure and ground have shifted.

Diagram 3.2 *Figure-ground applied to characters*

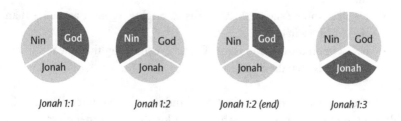

Jonah 1:1	*Jonah 1:2*	*Jonah 1:2 (end)*	*Jonah 1:3*

Characters in stories tend to form figures. They direct the attention of the reader and make all the other elements in the story, such as time, place, and objects, part of the ground. It is only when an unusual element in that ground appears that the reader's eye may shift, momentarily or longer depending on the extent of the surprise. In Jonah's story, the fish fulfills such a role (Jonah 2:1). For a brief moment the reader is caught up by this strange creature that swallows the prophet. Jonah stays in the fish for three days and three nights, which makes the reader ponder the nature of this animal. But just as the reader begins to wonder and ponder, the narrator ends the distraction by having Jonah pray to God (Jonah 2:2-10) and then having the fish vomit Jonah on the shore (Jonah 2:11). The story now returns to its initial focus: God and his prophecy (Jonah 3:1-3). The fish is ground, Jonah is ground too, and God is the figure.

Diagram 3.3 *Figure-ground in the fish episode*

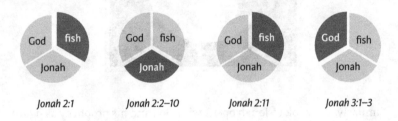

| Jonah 2:1 | Jonah 2:2–10 | Jonah 2:11 | Jonah 3:1–3 |

Figures share certain characteristics. Peter Stockwell (2002, 15) mentions the following:

- it [i.e., the figure] will be regarded as a self-contained object or feature in its own right, with well-defined edges separating it from the ground;
- it will be moving in relation to the static ground;
- it will precede the ground in time and space;
- it will be a part of the ground that has broken away, or emerges to become the figure;
- it will be more detailed, better focused, brighter or more attractive than the rest of the field;
- it will be on top of, or in front of, or above, or larger than the rest of the field that is then the ground.

The term "object" in this definition should not be taken too literally. In addition to real objects, such as the ship in Jonah 1, any other element in a story can function as a figure, and thus as the "object" or "feature" in the definition. Think of the already mentioned characters (e.g., Jonah or God), but also places (e.g., Nineveh) and time (e.g., forty days until Nineveh's overturning). In addition, stories have more levels on which "self-contained objects" can be distinguished. Let us return to the examples present in the short summary of the book of Jonah in the introduction of this chapter. Chapter 2, at least minus the introductory and ending sentence, forms a figure against the preceding and following chapter. Its overall style is very different from the narrative of chapters 1, 3, and 4. Scholars have called this a psalm, even one that alludes to the present psalter. Chapter 2 draws the reader's attention due to its different genre and style. It foregrounds Jonah's inner world and his personal struggle against the background of his physical journey. This is an example of figure-ground dynamics following changes in genre throughout the book.

Diagram 3.4 *Figure-ground applied to chapters of Jonah*

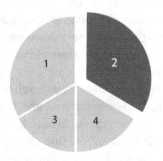

Chapter 2 vs. Other Chapters

Figure and ground also work on a smaller scale, with literary devices emphasizing important themes, protagonists, or other elements in the story. The highlighted items form figures, the rest of the story ground. These devices include features such as **chiasm** and **metaphor**. Each of them breaks through the unmarked way of speaking, creating a temporary deviation.[2] All languages have unmarked and marked ways of constructing sentences and phrases. The unmarked way is found in the majority of phrases. Hence, it will not draw attention when used. Marked phrasing, by contrast, is less frequent and there-

2. Note that these features appear in both everyday speech and literary language. The alternation between marked and unmarked language characterizes all language, regardless of mode or genre. Some genres, such as poetry, are known for using marked language more frequently, as do some speakers or writers.

fore stands out. *Markedness* can be found on virtually every level of language: the level of word order (as played with in chiasm), the level of choice of words (rare words for example), the level of images (metaphors), etc. To illustrate this with a few examples, look at the following passage from Jonah 2:6–7:

> [6] (They) *encompassed* me, the waters, as far as the throat;
> the deep *surrounded* me.
> Weeds bound around my head.
> [7] To the base of the mountains *I went down*;
> the earth, her bars (closed) behind me forever.
> Yet *you brought up* from the pit my life,
> Lord my God!

In the first two lines, the phrases have *chiastic constructions*: the initial verb-subject order ("encompassed"-"the waters") is followed by a subject-verb sequence ("the deep"-"surrounded"). The unusual word order forms a figure in the text, drawing the reader's attention to the content of the passage. There is an awful lot of water in these two lines. Moreover, the chiasm has the verbs ("encompassed" and "surrounded") enclose the water ("the waters" and "the deep") and the prophet's being ("the throat"), thus iconically closing in on them as well as on the reader. The reader pays full attention to the verbal actions of the water—the figure, whereas the prophet Jonah in the very middle of the verse becomes an element in the background. Verse 7 showcases another strong chiasm with Jonah's sinking and God's bringing up. These two verbs, semantic antonyms, are joined, but more importantly the reversed word order connects the lowest and highest point, encircling the verbs: the base of the mountains and God. As readers we move, as with a camera, from the bottom to the very top. It is at the top that our gaze rests, with God (figure). In these phrases, although Jonah is the speaker and he is relating his experience, his position is less important. Overall, he is the ground against which nature (waters and mountains) and ultimately God form the figures.

Diagram 3.5 *Figure-ground in Jonah 2*

The metaphor THE EARTH IS A HOUSE in verse 7 generates another figure, once more drawing attention away from Jonah (ground) to the earth (figure) this time. The earth is presented as having bars, a term typically used for houses (with doors to be locked) and cities (with gates to be closed). Obviously, the earth is neither one of them. Closed in by the water, Jonah is locked out of the dry land, the place where human life thrives. In verses 6 and 7 Jonah himself matters less and less. Full attention is given to the elements of nature and their devastating power.

Both examples—with chiasm and metaphor—illustrate how literary devices render what they emphasize into figures and what is surrounding these devices into grounds. As is clear from the examples, the focus can be on characters, such as Jonah, but also on actions or elements of nature.

In the discussion of figure and ground, Lesley Jeffries and Dan McIntyre argue that two processes can generate figures: *deviation*, as discussed above, and **parallelism**. Whereas deviation involves "violation[s] or departure[s] from certain linguistic norms," parallelism is an "unexpected repetition of such norms" (Gregoriou 2009, 27). In biblical poetry, however, parallelism is the main mode of composition, just like meter is in other languages. In other words, parallelism in biblical poetry can be considered the unmarked way of writing, and thus by definition creating grounds rather than figures. It is chiasm—the violation of the pattern—that produces figures, as in the word order shift in the examples above. At the same time, though, parallelism draws the reader's attention, and thus generates a figure, at the very beginning of a poetic section, as in Jonah 2, where it contrasts with the narrative mode used before in chapter 1 and the first verse of chapter 2. And parallelism forms a figure after a passage with chiasms, where it is the parallel structure that differs from the chiastic one. In other words, the use of parallelism and chiasm in biblical poetry forms an excellent example of the dynamic nature of figure and ground in the reading process. In addition, parallelism in narrative text, such as chapters 1, 3, and 4 of the book of Jonah, creates figures as well. Repeated structures are unexpected there. The end of chapter 4 forms a good example of that.

[10] Then the LORD said:
"*You cared about* the plant,
which you did not work for and
    which you did not *make great*,
which appeared overnight and
    perished overnight.

[11] And *I should not care about* Nineveh,
    that *great* city
    in which there are more than a hun-
        dred and twenty thousand people
    who do not know their right hand
        from their left
    and many beasts?"

Verses 10 (minus the introductory statement) and 11 are composed in a parallel way. Both open with a personal pronoun ("you" in verse 10 and "I" in verse 11) followed by the same verb and a prepositional phrase. Note that, contrary to English, Biblical Hebrew does not need to express subjects when they are personal pronouns because they are included in the verbal form. Explicitly mentioning personal pronouns emphasizes the subject. In this particular case, doing this twice draws attention to the parallelism between both verses. The parallel structure also continues after the first line with two relative clauses introduced by "which" in verse 10 and by "in which" and "who" in verse 11. Again, the parallelism is even stronger in the Hebrew source text because there is only one relative pronoun (*asher*), used in all but one place here, and a less frequently used by-form (*she*). In addition, there are repeated roots, such as in the verb "to make great" (*gadal*, v. 10) and the adjective "great" (*gedolah*, v. 11), and similar sounding words for "overnight" (*ben laylah*, v. 10) and "from" (*ben*, v. 11). All of these "unexpected repetitions," to refer to the earlier definition, catch the reader's attention and foreground the similarity between Jonah's relation to the plant and God's relation to Nineveh. Possible differences disappear in the background, even though many a commentator has written about them. Such is not surprising because the parallel structure does not coincide with parallel content. For one, the underlying rhetorical argument is not a proper parallelism, but *a minus ad maiore argument*: if something counts for a small matter, it definitely counts for something big. Thus, if Jonah cares about something as futile as a single plant with a short life, the more should God care about something as big as the city of Nineveh which is ancient. Secondly, the verse about Jonah is a statement whereas the lines about God are a rhetorical question with a negation. Should God not care? The answer is obviously that he should! Scholarship has labeled the contrast in content between the verse about Jonah and the verse about God as *antiparallelism*. And thirdly, verse 11 actually lacks a semantic parallel for most of verse 10, namely that God worked for Nineveh (vs. Jonah did not work for the plant) and that it was an ancient city (vs. the plant had a short lifespan). Although scholars have listed all these differences, all of them are grounds against the following figure: that God's position can be understood in light of Jonah's experience. In other words, the narrator explains God's reasoning through a comparison with Jonah's thinking.

Short History

Visual arts and Gestalt psychology first introduced the concepts figure and ground. Human beings experience the world around them by distinguishing boundaries of objects and categorizing them as figures against their back-grounded settings. Very often the introduction of the concept is accompanied by the so-called Rubin's vase, named after Edgar Rubin who first published the image in his doctoral thesis in 1915. If the viewer focuses on the black part in the image, this comes to the foreground, appearing as a vase. Alternatively, the viewer can focus on the white part, seeing two faces instead of the vase. One single viewer can shift his attention from one to the other, going back and forth between vase and face, or making the vase and face switch their roles of figure and ground (called a Gestalt switch by psychologists). However, at no point can the viewer see both at the same time. In other words, the concept of figure requires a concept of ground and vice versa.

Diagram 3.6 *Vase-face image*

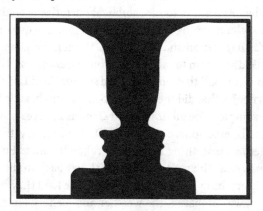

This visual experience of figure and ground has engraved a pattern in our thinking so that we apply the same process also to nonvisual objects such as characters in a story or a novel metaphor in a text. Each time the process is the same: we discern a figure, something that draws our attention and to which we consequently attribute importance; the rest disappears in the background. When we read a text, this process constantly repeats. It guides us through the text. Sometimes we may pick up cues that the writer has left there for us in-tentionally—think of an extraordinary element such as the plant God gives to Jonah at the end of the book (Jonah 4:6). Other times, we may focus on things that the-writer may not have intended for us to spend too much time on. Poetic verse in the Hebrew Bible draws on parallelism, a mode that readers with a different set of poetic keys may perceive as figure. Yet, in the poetic books of the Hebrew Bible, parallelism may be less significant for reader attention than we tend to think. Obviously, changes in the pattern will be meaningful. In any case, the aim of the presented figure-ground analysis, as of the other pieces in the book, is not to unravel the intention of the writer(s), but to track how readers make sense of a text, regardless of a writer's intentions.

Related Features in Biblical Studies

The notions of *foreground* and *background* in combination with style are probably best known in biblical studies as labels introduced by Erich Auerbach in the chapter "Odysseus' Scar" in his work *Mimesis: Dargestellte Wirklichkeit in der abenländischen Literatur* (1946). In this chapter, Auerbach compares two pieces of world literature, the Old Testament and the *Odyssey*, and their respective styles. According to him, biblical narrative is characterized by a **background style**, meaning that it abounds in gaps and questions and relies on the reader's imagination and interaction. What is Abraham thinking and feeling when God asks him to sacrifice his son in Genesis 22? Did Sarah agree that Abraham would kill their long-awaited son for God? Did she know at all about the journey? What did the scenery look like on this trip? How was the weather, for example? The biblical text of Genesis 22 reveals almost nothing in terms of details, emotions, or thoughts. On the contrary, the **foreground style** of Homer leaves nothing unspoken. When the maid Eurykleia recognizes Odysseus's scar, the reader travels with her back to the day Odysseus got that scar. Everything is described in detail: the food they had at the banquet and how it was prepared, the weather and scenery on the morning of the hunt, how a wild boar injured Odysseus, and how they took care of the wound. The writer also pays ample attention to the emotions of characters. For example, Eurykleia is first scared then happy and sad at the same time, when she recognizes her master. Readers learn about this both through literal mentioning of it and through her behavior (her eyes fill with tears, her voice falters). Auerbach's labels of foreground and background concern the writing style of the works as a whole rather than how elements within one work relate and move against one another, which is how foreground and background are understood in more recent studies. However, both share the idea that textual style influences the reading process and experience.

In addition, biblical scholars have studied the notion of **foregrounding** and its resultant effect of **defamiliarization**, both from a literary and a linguistic point of view. Following the former, foregrounding concerns the narrative or poetic structure and the literary sophistication of the text. For example, the word "great" is repeated at various places in the book of Jonah. It ensures the unity of the story and works as an anchor point for the reader. In linguistic studies, the foregrounded element deviates from the standard grammatical norms, such as a reversed word order or unusual tense use.

Lastly, researchers have analyzed **stylistic figures** in the biblical text. They include, among others, chiasm, **alliteration**, and metaphor. The majority of these devices have been studied within a literary-poetic framework, in which the features are understood as contributing to the literary character of the text. For metaphor, scholars have also turned more recently to cognitive linguistics and its insights in the way in which our mind categorizes and understands the world and our experiences through metaphor (more on metaphor in chapter 8).

The Meaning of Figure and Ground in Biblical Studies

The previous section illustrates that scholars, as other readers, pay attention to figures naturally when reading and interpreting the Bible. The incorporation of the ground aspect and the dynamics between figure and ground in these readings can further enrich our understanding of the biblical text. Self-evidently, the foregrounded element, thus the figure, is still the part that draws our attention and is endowed with significance, but where did it come from and where does it go as the story progresses? What is backgrounded when this figure appears? And what is the relationship between figure and ground?

More generally, figure and ground allow us to track the focus of a text. Researchers can take this focus into account when establishing their research questions. Some questions in particular will benefit from a figure-ground analysis. Think of questions about silencing certain voices in the text, for example, those of women, children, exiles, and the people as collective. In the famous story of David and Bathsheba in 2 Samuel 11, figure and ground can shed new light on Bathsheba's position in the story as well as on the dynamics with David. When does the reader focus on her, that is, when does she become a figure in the text? What is the husband's position in this schema? And how is all of this achieved textually? Also questions regarding dominant stylistic features of the biblical text, such as parallelism, can be analyzed anew with figure and ground. When and how are parallelisms broken? How does the reader's eye move in biblical poetry where various elements may qualify as figures? And what forms the ground in these texts? In biblical narrative, it is possible to follow a certain character through its positions as figure or ground. When do changes occur? Do these different positions involve character development as well?

Because figure and ground are such basic concepts, they will be relevant for almost any type of research conducted on the text and any type of reading of that text. The theologian can track the position of God throughout a text, the anthropologist that of the exile. For the structuralist, the recurring of certain figure-ground combinations may be interesting, while the redactional critic can benefit from figure-ground analysis in determining how much of the redactional stitching is brought under the reader's attention. The ecological researcher will have a way of deciding nature's role in the text, and a postmodernist will question the importance of the figure and the insignificance of the ground.

Case Study: Figure-Ground Analysis of Jonah's Message to Nineveh

To illustrate the relevance of the figure-ground concept for biblical studies further, let us turn to the book of Jonah one more time. The book features Jonah and God as prominent characters, but there is also the city of Nineveh and its inhabitants. They form the object of the prophecy and dominate most of chapter 3. However, many researchers have paid little to no attention to the role of the city in the story, limiting it to the overall reversal theme of the book: a bad city is presented as a good one. Whereas that is one way to understand the city's role in the book, a figure-ground analysis shows that there is more to it. Or rather, the city itself has a voice too in the text and reading its story does not only enrich the current understanding of the book of Jonah; it may also change, or at least question, some of the generally accepted claims about the book.

JONAH 3:1–10

[1] And the word of the LORD came to Jonah a second time: [2] *"Get up, go to Nineveh, the great city,* and announce *to it* the announcement that I tell you." [3] And Jonah *got up and went to Nineveh* following the word of the LORD. And Nineveh was a mighty *great city, a walk of three days across.*

⁴ And Jonah started *to come into* the *city, one day's walk,* and he announced and said: "Forty more days and *Nineveh* shall be overthrown/overthrow itself!" ⁵ And the people of *Nineveh* believed God. And they announced a fast, and they dressed in sackcloth, from great to small.

⁶ And the word reached the king of *Nineveh,* and he rose from his throne, and took off his mantle from himself. And he covered with sackcloth and sat in the dust. ⁷ And he called together and said in *Nineveh:* "By decree of the king and his great men: Human and animal, cow or sheep, they shall not taste anything. They shall not graze, and they shall not drink water. ⁸ And they shall be covered with sackcloth, human and animal, and they shall cry to God with strength. And they shall return, each, from their evil path and from the wrongdoing that is in their hands. ⁹ Who knows, God may turn and relent. And he may return from his anger, so that we do not perish."

¹⁰ And God saw their deeds, that they returned from their evil path. And God regretted the evil he had said to do to them, and he did not do it.

Nineveh draws the reader's full attention in chapter 3 of the book of Jonah. In the first lines of the chapter (vv. 1–4), various elements in the text emphasize Nineveh. There are repeated spatial references, such as the keyword "great" (two times), the word "city" (three times), and the name of the city (four times). In addition, directional prepositions, such as "to" and motion verbs, such as "get up" and "go, walk" (vv. 2–3) draw further attention to Nineveh. The reader, together with Jonah, is looking at this city that appears as a figure, an elevated center. This position changes radically after verse 4. The verse in which Jonah's prophecy about overthrowing appears also announces a stylistic overturning. Prepositions and motion verbs express removal and descent from now on. There is no longer lexical repetition in the text, except for one passage, and no further mention of the word "city." The name of the city occurs only three times in verses 5–10, a passage that is far longer than the four opening verses of the chapter. All these interventions move Nineveh to a position of ground in the narrative. The city is no longer important. What we see is a more modest space/character with a lower and less central position.

Note that the only repetition in this second part of the narrative concerns the return from an evil path (vv. 8, 10). The repetition emphasizes the removal of the Ninevites. Additionally, the phrase focuses on the individual rather than the collective, thus also decentralizing the city's power and position. Furthermore, the people are not called Ninevites but persons. By not naming them explicitly, the city is once again forced to the background. Or better, the people execute this act themselves. They initiate actions (fasting, sitting in dust, wearing sackcloth) that turn their foregrounded position into one in the background. In doing so, they hope that God will leave his initial position toward them as well (vv. 8–9) and will no longer see a cause for destroying the city. At the end of chapter 3, the spatial dynamics between figure and ground are set right, with God as figure and the space of the Ninevites as ground.

The above analysis, drawing on figure-ground dynamics, offers insight in the position of the city in the book of Jonah. With the findings in mind, it also prompts the question whether God truly saved Nineveh. The text of Jonah presents a prominent city at the beginning, followed by a prophecy of reversal and by actions by the city to change their foregrounded position. The stylistic changes also impact our reading of the city: figure means importance, ground equals insignificance. As a result of this change in position, Nineveh is no longer a threat, there is no further need for God to intervene. The Ninevites have destroyed themselves, so to speak, with their "overturning" or backgrounding. Yet, at the same time this turn also saved their lives in the story world.

Ideas for Discussion

1. Continue the example of figure-ground dynamics at the beginning of the chapter with the characters in Jonah 1. Which characters draw most of the attention in this chapter, and are thus figures? Which characters function mostly as ground?

2. Select a passage from the remaining chapters of the book of Jonah and track one of the main characters (God or Jonah) as figure/ground. When do changes in their position occur? How are they marked in the text? Look, for example, for prepositions, subject or object function in the sentence, and literary devices.

3. Relying on figure-ground dynamics, can you explain the role of the captain in chapter 1, the king in chapter 3, and the plant in chapter 4? And what is the position of the silent voices of the sailors and the Ninevites?

4. After having looked at all these different characters, we can move to the themes of the book of Jonah. How does a figure-ground analysis assist in assessing the focus and message of the book of Jonah? Is it a book about a wandering prophet, or rather about a God who watches over anybody regardless of location and even faith? In other words, who is the figure in the story as a whole? And does a figure-ground analysis support your initial ideas about the text?

5. Think of other prophetic books, such as Amos or Isaiah. Read a small excerpt

and track the position of the prophet in these texts. Is the prophet the ground or the figure? When does it change? Do the same for a small excerpt of Samuel or Kings (for example, Saul at Endor in 1 Samuel 28 or Elisha's miracles in 2 Kings 4). Which of the patterns shows most resemblance with the figure-ground dynamics in the book of Jonah and the position of the prophet therein?

6. Can you think of other biblical books or stories in which a character (or space or object) is clearly the figure? How is this achieved textually, that is, how does the language of the text make the reader come to this conclusion?

Further Reading

For an introduction of foregrounding in language and literature, consult Peter Stockwell, *Cognitive Poetics: An Introduction* (2002), and Peter Stockwell, "Surreal Figures" (2003). In addition, the following works also offer accessible introductions: Lesley Jeffries and Dan McIntyre, *Stylistics* (2010), and Christiana Gregoriou, *English Literary Stylistics* (2009).

The origin of the concept is discussed in Edgar Rubin, *Synsoplevede Figurer* (1915); Rudolf Arnheim, *Art and Visual Perception* (1957); and David C. Beardslee and Max Wertheimer, *Readings in Perception* (1958).

Studies of related features in biblical studies are Erich Auerbach, *Mimesis: Dargestellte Wirklichkeit in der abenländischen Literatur* (1946); Wilfred Watson, *Classical Hebrew Poetry: A Guide to Its Techniques* (1984); Meir Sternberg, *The Poetics of Biblical Narrative: Ideological Literature and the Drama of Reading* (1985); Robert Alter, *The Art of Biblical Poetry* (1985); Jean-Marc Heimerdinger, *Topic, Focus and Foreground in Ancient Hebrew Narratives* (1999); Stefano Cotrozzi, *Expect the Unexpected: Aspects of Pragmatic Foregrounding in Old Testament Narrative* (2010); Peter W. Macky, *The Centrality of Metaphors to Biblical Thought: A Method for Interpreting the Bible* (1990); and Pierre Van Hecke, *Metaphor in the Hebrew Bible* (2005).

Finally, a short selection of relevant studies on the book of Jonah are Phyllis Trible, *Rhetorical Criticism: Context, Method, and the Book of Jonah* (1994); Ehud Ben Zvi, *Signs of Jonah: Reading and Rereading in Ancient Yehud* (2003); and Karolien Vermeulen, "Save or Sack the City: The Fate of Jonah's Nineveh from a Spatial Perspective" (2017).

FOUR

Perspective and Pointing the Way

Deixis

Who's Talking Now?

Human communication is a fascinating and multivalent phenomenon. It ranges from gestures—a raised eyebrow, an uplifted hand, shrugged shoulders, facial expressions of all sorts—to oral communication—speaking, singing, yelling, moaning, cheering, ordering, acquiescing—to written communication—books, pamphlets, documents, decrees, candy wrappers, and constitutions. Face-to-face communication is one of the most ordinary of human activities, yet one with huge ramifications. Often speaker status determines who is heard and who is ignored, whose words are written down and remembered, and whose are neglected and forgotten. For this reason, one of the most important questions to ask when reading the Bible is: "Who's talking now?" Many theological readers hold to the presupposition that God is the ultimate speaker, while other readers look to the author or narrator as the primary speaker for the text. In any case, it is necessary to sort out whose perspective is being represented: is it the author of a book, the narrator, one of the characters? How are the speaker's words used to represent their immediate situation of speaking? For, just as the reader of the biblical text is in conversation with the text and its writers, the narrator and characters in the text are portrayed as being in conversation with one another. Sorting out the perspectives represented by these layers of communication and understanding the situations laid out in the text is part of reading well. We want to know who is talking, and what is their angle on the events in the text.

All about Perspective

For readers of the biblical text, understanding **perspective** can provide further understanding of the constraints of the text and its message. Perspective, whether in conversation or in written text, includes notions such as **viewpoint** (whose eyes are we looking through?) and **deixis** (where are we in physical and conceptual space?). Because perspective is firmly anchored to characterization in written text, both viewpoint and deixis are related to the social roles and location of the characters in a text, including the sometimes-obscure narrator. In complicated terms, the idea of perspective includes presenting "a subjective point of view that restricts the validity of information" to a certain person or character in a discourse (Sanders and Redeker 1996, 293). Thus, speaking characters can become the **deictic center**, or reference point in each portion of text. This in turn restricts the validity of the information they provide: The information provided via a character's perspective may be limited and constrained by his or her location in time, space, and culture. For example, such information may be true, but not be valid in the larger trajectory of the Scriptures. Job's three friends stand out in this regard. Upon observing Job's suffering, each of the friends speaks to Job with words meant to explain the "why" of the situation. They say things about God that appear to be true, but as God states in Job 42:7b, ". . . you have not spoken of me what is right, as my servant Job has" (NRSV). In effect, their words are true on one level, but are not valid in this situation.

There are three interrelated thoughts that can contribute to understanding the valuable role deixis plays in establishing perspective in both spoken and written communication. First, deixis is a feature of a *situation of speaking*, a situation that is marked by the presence of speaker, hearer, and a message, all of which are foregrounded against the **ground** of the situation. Secondly, deixis is a type of reference that uses speaker-related elements in a speech situation to designate something in a scene. For example, if several people are seated around the dining room table and person A says, "Pass me *that* hot buttered bread roll," the situation of speaking presupposes that there are two or more people located within earshot of one another, along with a hot buttered bread roll that is within eyesight and within reach of at least two of them. Moreover, the term "me" indicates that the statement is pictured (or **construed**) from person A's perspective. Person A is the deictic center. If person B replies, "This one?" the viewpoint shifts, and person B becomes the deictic center—the situation is construed from person B's perspective. In this example, the near demonstrative "this" implies that person B is in closer proximity to the hot buttered bread rolls than person A. The hot buttered bread roll's role as "this roll" or "that roll" is based on which person is speaking. This shows how deixis is anchored to a specific speaker within a situation of speaking. If our diner had said, "Please give me a hot buttered roll," the roll could be in the kitchen, the living room, or out on the porch. It is the speaker's use of the deictic or pointing term "this" or "that" that anchors the hot buttered bread roll to the immediate situation of speaking: it is a specific roll, one within pointing distance and within view of all speech participants in the situation. Finally, the dependence upon the character's perspective within the situation of speaking means that the speech situation is inherently subjective, as opposed to the quasi-objective construal exhibited by narrative text.

All about Deixis

Since deixis proper is a function that (1) takes place within a situation of speaking, and (2) uses speaker-related elements to designate something in a scene, it is helpful to examine the characteristics of some common (prototypical) and uncommon (non-prototypical) speech situations.

A variety of possible speech situations are found in diagram 4.1, which has a prototypical situation at the center of the diagram. The prototypical situation of speaking includes at least two entities who take turns as speaker/hearer, and a message. The situation of speaking is grounded in both time and space and the participants likely share a certain amount of cultural background. The "breakfast at home" speech situation includes at least two participants involved in a synchronous communication, with a shared location and shared social context. The coffee shop situation includes at least two participants, is synchronous, and features a shared location and shared social context. The chat on the street is also synchronous and in a shared location; however, the social context may be less specific. These three situations closely resemble the prototypical situation, creating a conversation "script" that is expected and easily shared. The next two examples veer away from the prototype in various ways and can be considered non-prototypical situations. The now-ubiquitous "2020 Zoom Meet-up" shares the synchronous nature of the prototypical situation, and generally shares some social context. Notably, what causes the Zoom meeting to veer away from the prototype is the non-shared physical space. As weary Zoomers note, chatting in a Zoom room misses out on useful information and social cues. Pushing the mute button is foreign to normal conversation and can cause further distancing. Surprisingly and significantly, reading also veers away from the prototype in meaningful ways, showing that reading the Bible as a communication event presents certain challenges. Simply stated, as conversation partners go, the present-day reader and the originator of the biblical text are distanced by time, location, and non-shared social contexts.

Diagram 4.1 *Prototypical and non-prototypical situations of speaking*

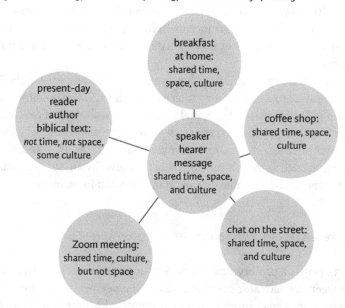

Human communication can be a prototypical face-to-face interaction, or non-prototypical interaction mediated through technology or books. However, all situations share embodied human experience, and it is because of this shared experience that present-day readers can be on the same page as the ancient writers. We all derive information about the world through our senses, making image schemas, scripts, and frames available across time and culture. The ubiquity of human speech as a framing device is one powerful example of this.

Because reading a text is a non-prototypical communication event, deixis—using speaker-related elements to designate something in a scene—functions on more than one level. First, there is the level of the text originator (author, editor, redactor) and the reader. Clearly there is much to be discussed regarding the various originators of the text, but for now we will look at them as a general category and at "the reader" as another general category. This level is called the *discourse level*. The discourse level, or discourse world, is the point of contact between the real world and the world(s) of the text (see chapters 10 and 12).

The biblical text itself is the second level. The biblical text is filled with speech of all sorts: reported speech, direct speech, indirect speech, reported perception such as seeing and hearing, thinking, feeling, believing, and so forth. Various situations of speaking are embedded within the text, sometimes in multiple layers at the *text level* as part of the text world (see chapter 12). We will discuss the bigger picture in future chapters, but for now we will look at several examples of text-level deixis to get to know more about deixis proper.

There are several types of deixis that can be identified linguistically. For example, we can scan a text for *deictic terms*, which include words from the semantic domains of person, time, and space. The vocabulary of deixis also includes proper names, personal pronouns—terms that indicate the character's perspective within the text, demonstrative pronouns such as "this" and "that," locative adverbs such as "near" and "far," temporal adverbs such as "yesterday" and "today" and, when available, temporal information in verbal forms.

Example 1: Person Deixis in Matthew 3:13–15

Matthew 3:13-15 is a prototypical example of reported speech. The passage moves between the narrator's perspective and the perspectives of John and Jesus. The narrator's voice introduces the communication event between John and Jesus at 3:13, stating: "Then Jesus came from Galilee to John at the Jordan, to be baptized by him" (NRSV). At 3:14a, the narrator continues: "John would have prevented him, *saying*." Here the term "saying" introduces John's words in 14:b as reported speech—John says to Jesus: "I need to be baptized by you, and do you come to me?" At 3:15a, the narrator adds another indicator of reported speech: "But Jesus *answered* him," followed by Jesus's reply to John in 15b, "Let it be so now; for it is proper for us in this way to fulfill all righteousness." The narrator's voice ends the paragraph with the statement at 15c: "Then he consented." This short example shows how the narrator represents a situation of speaking, placing important content into the voices of the speaking characters who are presented as having a prototypical conversation. We are less aware of how the narrator may be feeling about the situation as the narrator's voice is using third-person style to report the situation. We are much more aware of John's incredulous response to Jesus's upending his expectations about who should be baptizing whom and of Jesus's confident response, mainly because these statements are in the form of "you and I," first and second person conversation.

Example 2: Epistemic Deixis, a Subset of Person Deixis in Jeremiah 3:6–7

Prophetic literature is slightly more complex to deal with, as the situation of speaking at both the discourse level and the text level is non-prototypical. In Jeremiah 3, this situation is quite clear: Jeremiah claims to be on speaking terms with God. The validity of this claim is well grounded in prior chapters, particularly in Jeremiah's call narrative in Jeremiah 1. Because Jeremiah and God are presented as conversation partners in this text, we are invited to see things from God's perspective. This is accomplished via *epistemic deixis*, where perception terms, such as seeing, hearing, and thinking, allow the reader a peek at life from a character's internal perspective, including their mind, will, and emotions. All of this to say, having a conversation with the deity is less prototypical than having a coffee chat with a friend (see diagram 4.1).

Jeremiah's first-person report of his conversation in chapter 3 begins with the introductory verse at 3:6: "The LORD said to me in the days of King Josiah: Have you seen what she did, that faithless one, Israel, how she went up on every high hill and under every green tree, and played the whore there?" (NRSV). God is clearly not pleased with Israel at this point and seems to be venting to Jeremiah. The account deepens at 3:7a where the epistemic deictic phrase, "And *I thought*" is followed by God's hopeful "After she has done all this she will return to me." But this retrospective also includes the disappointed observation: "but she did not return, and her false sister Judah saw it."

Further examples of person, time, and location deixis are discussed in the longer example below.

Short History

The 1980s brought a rise in cognitive studies from a variety of perspectives. Grammarians such as Ronald Langacker revisited and reimagined grammar from a cognitive perspective. Frank Brisard brought together a number of cognitive linguistics essays in his volume, *Grounding: The Epistemic Footing of Deixis and Reference*, including Langacker's study, "Deixis and Subjectivity." Scholars such as Sanders and Redeker explored the relationship between perspective and the way that speech and thought are represented in narrative discourse.

Related Features in Biblical Studies

Point of view, characterization, and perspective are three aspects of the text that are of interest to biblical studies. Point of view involves discovering whose eyes we are looking through when reading a particular text. This is established by looking at who is doing the speaking, for point of view is a subjective aspect of the text, based on its connection to the narrator or the character. This makes characterization an equally important aspect of the text: Who are the main characters? Are they reliable? Do they speak the truth, or are they like Job's friends who speak the truth but do so in a manner that isn't right? This will affect the point of view taken in each text. With this information in mind, a reader can think more clearly about how his or her point of view lines up with that of the author, narrator, or character in a text.

The Meaning of Perspective and Deixis in Biblical Studies

Given their importance for interpretation, ascertaining perspective and deixis in the text is an important aspect of biblical studies. Perspective, including viewpoint, helps to situate the text in time, space, and culture, and this information is very important for accurate exegesis and actualization in modern times and cultures. Deixis allows the reader and interpreter to evaluate the subjective point of view of given speakers and characters, and this helps to better understand the validity of the information presented in each text. For example, as mentioned above, in the case of Job's friends, the information they shared with Job was true, but it was not valid for Job's situation (see p. 55).

Establishing perspective and deixis is a function of the author in the first instance; however, we do not have direct access to the author to double check their meaning and intention. In fact, the narrator is the more reliable voice in a text, and it is the narrator who sorts out and presents the voices and situations of the characters. For that reason, even though a character speaks in a more direct way, what is being said or not said is being directed by the narrator.

The book of Psalms appears to be a different challenge in this regard, and it is worth looking at how the consistent use of the "I-Thou" pair in the Psalms creates the impression of intimacy and closeness with the original speaker. It also creates a nearly inevitable interpretive leap for the present-day reader: who does not refer to themselves as "I"? It is very easy to identify with the speaker in the Psalms; however, it is imperative to keep in mind that these are ancient texts written in a very different time, place, and culture. A deliberate review of the ancient context is important to avoid this interpretive leap. In the case of the Psalms, superscriptions provide deictic information regarding time, space, and culture in many cases, which can be a good jumping-off point for such a review.

Case Study: Amos 1:1–5 and Beyond

The book of Amos contains some of the most clearly stated examples of person, location, and time deixis in the biblical text.

Amos 1:1 reads: "The words of **Amos**, who was among the **shepherds** of Tekoa, which he saw concerning Israel in the days of **King Uzziah** of Judah and in the days of **King Jeroboam** son of **Joash** of Israel, *two years before the earthquake*" (NRSV).

In this example, persons are marked in bold, locations are underlined, and the time margin is italicized. From this introductory statement, we see that Amos is the main character, that he was associated with the shepherds of Tekoa, and that he "saw" certain words regarding King Uzziah (Judah) and King Jeroboam (Israel). Unfortunately, the time margin, "two years before the earthquake" is far more ambiguous than it first seems, as the identity of the earthquake is not known.

Location deixis is an important aspect of the Amos text. At verse 2 Amos says: "The LORD roars from Zion, and utters his voice from Jerusalem; the pastures of the shepherds wither, and the top of Carmel dries up." By this we may understand that Amos is speaking on behalf of the LORD from Jerusalem. He is the deictic center for what follows: we see the following action from his perspective. The following prophetic oracles are arranged with both geography and rhetoric in mind. The series of judgment oracles are each introduced with the prophetic formula, "Thus says the LORD." Amos 1:3 announces judgment on Damascus, which is to the northeast of Jerusalem. Amos 1:6 mentions Gaza, which is to the southwest. This is followed by Amos 1:9 which speaks of Tyre, which is to the northwest. Amos 1:11 mentions Edom, to the southeast. Amos

1:13 announces judgment on Ammon, to the northeast, and Amos 2:1 addresses Moab to the southeast. The cumulative judgments grow in intensity and suddenly they circle back to Judah in Amos 2:4 and Israel in Amos 2:6. While the prophet's Israelite audience was probably nodding in agreement that God would judge the surrounding nations, it is easy to see them suddenly become quiet and anxious when they realize that they, too, are going to be judged.

Diagram 4.2 *Location deixis in Amos 1*

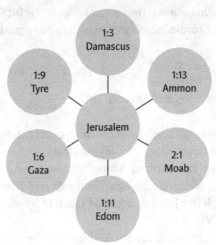

Ideas for Discussion

1. Read Jeremiah 1:1–3. What clues does the narrator offer regarding the times, locations, and characters in this section of text? What is the main time frame for Jeremiah's prophetic career in this section?
2. With the prior answers in mind, read Jeremiah 1:4–10. What times, locations, and characters are involved in this text? Does the text contain any time shifts between present, past, and future?

Further Reading

Deixis proper is a rather technical topic. In their volume *Spaces, Worlds, and Grammar* (1996), Gilles Fauconnier and Eve Sweetser have collected a number of readable essays on the topic. Two of the more approachable essays are "Perspective and the Representation of Speech and Thought in Narrative Discourse" (1996) by José Sanders and Gisela Redeker and "Alternate Grounds in the Interpretation of Deictic Expressions" (1996) by Jo Rubba. A second group of essays are included in Keith Green, *New Essays in Deixis: Discourse, Narrative, Literature* (1995). Finally another worthy essay is "Deixis and Subjectivity," in *Grounding: The Epistemic Footing of Deixis and Reference* (Brisard 2002).

Deixis is also an important aspect of cognitive grammar (see chapter 5). The topic is well discussed in Ronald W. Langacker, *Concept, Image, and Symbol: The Cognitive Basis of Grammar* (2002). There is also an interest in Lesley Jeffries and Dan McIntyre, *Stylistics* (2010).

FIVE

Grammar and Cognitive Grammar

Talking about Language

Describing the Language of Scripture

The way we read the Bible is both similar and different to the way we read any written text. On the surface, it appears to be much the same—English readers peruse the text from left to right whether it is presented as a conventional book or as a Kindle version, whether it is Scripture or a novel. While in the back of our minds we have some vague notions of parts of speech, such as nouns and verbs, we rarely stop to identify the term "Yahweh" as a proper noun or account for God's action in the phrase "in the beginning, God *created*" as a verbal form. However, as any beginning student of biblical languages soon learns, talking about language, grammar in particular, is a necessary part of moving from Greek or Hebrew to English or another target language. Translation highlights the need for a common language to talk about language, from individual words, to clauses, to sentences—and on to whole paragraphs. In order to describe how these levels fit together, linguists speak of semantics, syntax, and grammar from a multitude of perspectives. Cognitive grammar is one such perspective.

All about Cognitive Grammar

Broadly speaking, grammar highlights the distinction between categories such as nouns, verbs, and relation words (little words such as "and," "but," and "if"). This is done in a variety of ways, depending upon the mode of approach. While traditional grammar is largely descriptive and is seen as an objective reality, cognitive grammar takes human experience as a starting point. It views grammatical categories as schematic and dependent upon the speaker or writer's **construal** of words, clauses, and sentences. Additionally, cognitive grammar fits well with the broader "cognitive turn," as it views communication as an embodied phenomenon. The context-driven nature of cognitive grammar is its most original claim. For example, a dictionary definition of the term "fight" includes entries for both a verb and a noun, both based upon application of force. A contextual example, such as 1 Timothy 6:12 shows how context is required to sort out the grammatical category of each of the two uses of "fight" in the phrase, "Fight the good fight of the faith" (NRSV) in the English translation. Although identical in form (in English), the grammatical function of the terms in this sentence is worked out by the reader via contextual clues such as expected verb-object word order.

Ronald Langacker (1999, 2001, 2002) laid the groundwork for a conceptual approach to grammatical categories with his observation that two broad categories exist: things (autonomous entities, including nouns and adjectives) and events (relational entities, including verbs and prepositions). Giovanelli and Harrison (2018) refine this contrast with four broad observations regarding the differences between nouns and verb archetypes. (They use the term "archetype" to refer to a single idea that underlies all examples or *instances* of the category. Other linguists speak of a type-instance dichotomy.) First, regarding composition, the archetype for nouns is material substance, while the archetype for verbs is energy transfer. In the case of nouns, it is rather easy to see how a material substance could be profiled as a figure against the ground of the situation described in a clause or sentence. Second, regarding time, the noun archetype demonstrates indefinite location while the verb archetype is bound in time. Third, regarding space, the noun archetype is bound in space while the verb archetype is dependent on the location of the participants. Finally, regarding conceptualization, the noun archetype is conceptually autonomous—we can think about an entity such as a dog without needing to create a background. However, the verb archetype is context dependent and in order to conceptualize the phrase "a dog jumped over a log," we need both the dog and the locational context that is created by the action of jumping over the log.

Construal in Cognitive Grammar

One claim of cognitive grammar is that a speaker or writer engages in profiling a word, clause, or sentence, by focusing attention on one aspect over another. This is called construal and the speaker or writer may utilize several methods to profile a word, including those that play with *figure-ground alignment*, such as the Jonah examples in chapter 3, **deixis** as described in chapter 4, and **image schemas** as well. These notions are at the center of cognitive grammar and are used in describing both grammatical categories and grammar in use.

Notions such as figure-ground, deixis, and image schemas are all associated with the experiential nature of language. Each of these construal operations include noticing how the human senses are involved in language production. Vision and hearing are both important to this process and the grammatical descriptions often use concepts taken from the physical experiences of seeing and hearing. We have briefly looked at the notion of figure-ground, which is based upon the visual field (see chapter 3). Human vision is constrained to 180 degrees, with eyes on the front of the face, and we can see much farther out into space than we can touch with our hands. Human hearing is a full 360-degree experience, with the ears placed at the sides of the head, and we can hear from much farther away than we can physically touch. Seeing and hearing are key for maneuvering through the world—whether the physical world, or by metaphorical extension, worlds created by reading a text.

The Role of Image Schemas

The CONTAINMENT SCHEMA and the SOURCE-PATH-GOAL SCHEMA are two image schemas, or "information packages," that we all depend upon at the subconscious level for many aspects of daily life. These images schemas are something that small babies discover before they can speak—given a cup and a ball, a baby will move the ball into the cup, out of the cup, into the cup, out of the cup, physically discovering the idea of in and out, which is the basis for the CONTAINMENT SCHEMA. When bored with that, the baby will fling both ball and cup overboard, discovering things about the SOURCE-PATH-GOAL SCHEMA. Cognitive grammar points out the relevance of image schemas for thinking about grammatical expressions. This includes understanding how these image schemas help with conceptualizing words and phrases. When Giovanelli and Harrison explain that the archetype for nouns comprises being a material substance that can be thought of independently of time, bound in space, and conceptually autonomous, it becomes clear that in general, nouns play on the CONTAINMENT SCHEMA.

Diagram 5.1 *Containment schema*

The red circle within the white box is a noun, but the red circle could be replaced with any number of nouns: a dog, a cat, a baboon, an elephant—all of these can be profiled against the background with no time reference, but with full awareness that they are bound to one area in space. And we can talk about the baboon or elephant or red circle without needing to create a background at all. There are, however, some nouns that require a bit more processing and we will talk about those in the following section.

Conceptualizing verbs is a different story right from the start. Giovanelli and Harrison (2018) note that verbs indicate energy transfer, that they are bound in time, that they are spatially dependent upon the location of the participants and are context dependent. For these reasons, the SOURCE-PATH-GOAL SCHEMA plays into understanding verbs. A simple representation is seen here:

Diagram 5.2 *Source-path-goal schema*

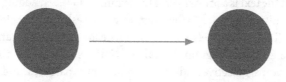

A sentence such as "The cat fell out of the tree" provides two nominals—the cat and the tree—which give the time-bound action of "falling" some spatial organization. Along with the little words "out of," the energy transfer of the falling body of the cat can be adequately profiled. The source is the treetop, the path is the downward energy transfer, and the (unfortunate) goal is the ground under the tree. The SOURCE-PATH-GOAL SCHEMA can also be seen in processing concepts such as time and space. A statement such as "Harold raced between 7:00 a.m. and 12:30 p.m." uses the SOURCE-PATH-GOAL SCHEMA by highlighting the beginning and endpoint of the race using temporal indicators, and the race is construed largely as a "path" across time. A statement such as "Harold raced from the Verrazano Bridge to Central Park" highlights the spatial aspects of the race, using the known start and endpoint for the New York City Marathon. In this sentence the race is construed in spatial terms, also using the SOURCE-PATH-GOAL SCHEMA. Moving from the bridge to the park, 26.2 miles are compressed into a path marked by two geographical points. Athletes will describe this type of course as an end to end race as opposed to an out and back circular course. These examples are simple instances of the role of image schemas; however, image schemas are sometimes used together. When a noun is not a simple count noun (dog, cat, baboon, or elephant) the issue of boundedness comes into play. Mass nouns such as water, air, and wind, and abstract nouns such as love, beauty, and truth are not as easily apprehended as referents with definite boundaries. And verbs may or may not show signs of boundedness in time.

Finally, because the verb archetype is context dependent on the participants, their presence becomes a rich source of deictic information. Terms such as "here" and "there" (spatial) and "then" and "now" (temporal) stated in a character's voice can be construed by that participant's location against the ground of a statement. His or her mind, will, and emotions may become available to the reader via verbs of perception and speech. Because of this, the depths of a text can be plumbed via the presence of the participants.

Traditional approaches to biblical text include grammatical studies that examine the text "for all it's worth." Such approaches are logical, as making sense of the grammar of the text is a primary clue to meaning. However, adding observations from a cognitive approach to the effort provides fresh categories for talking about the text. These categories are helpful for reader, language learner, and translator alike. Traditional grammatical descriptions refer to parts of speech such as nouns, verbs, adjectives, adverbs, conjunctions, particles, and so forth. These in turn are folded into categories such as subject, verb, and object. It is important to stay in touch with these terms, as many students of the biblical text are interested not only in the English versions, but the Greek and Hebrew text that underlies the translations. For those studying original languages, traditional categories are reflected in the textbooks, thus need to be understood and retained as ways of talking about language. Likewise, cognitive grammar can often give a boost to understanding what is going on in the original language text as well, because the traditional categories may not be sufficient for understanding language in use. It is a contrast between lexicon and usage event, with the usage event carrying enough context to disambiguate terms and constructions.

Talking about Grammar: Old Terms-New Terms

Where traditional grammar makes a primary distinction between nouns and verbs, cognitive grammar acknowledges a distinction between *things* and *events*. As we will see, the ability to categorize by usage event provides a few subcategories that provide helpful information to the reader.

Looking at nouns as nominals or "things" allows us to keep the idea of a term that refers to something that is a material substance, that can be thought of independently of time, that is bound in space, and is (on its own) conceptually autonomous. We can make a distinction between count nouns and mass nouns that proves to be conceptually important as well. Some nominals or "things" are countable: dogs, kittens, rocks, spoons, and ice cream cones can be lined up and counted. We can have one dog, a single kitten, forty-four rocks, or three ice cream cones. Each of these items is a material substance that can be thought of without reference to time and so forth. Mass nouns, on the other hand, such as water, ice cream, and sand are slightly different. While we can speak of "a puppy" or "the ice cream cone," we cannot get by with talking about "a water" or "the sand" without more contextual information, as they do not have natural edges—the ice cream needs the cone to become countable. Essentially, mass nouns are not easily countable on their own and are not as firmly bound in space. However, mass nouns are things, and things that are great for making metaphors, as we shall soon see.

Example 1: Israel

The proper noun "Israel" is a useful case study. In the biblical context, this term is used as both a count noun and as a quasi-mass noun. In all cases, it is a "thing." After wrestling with a divine being Jacob is renamed Israel, an instance of a single referent described with a proper noun. The term refers to a single person and thus is a count noun. But the plot thickens! Jacob/Israel had twelve sons who in turn produce the groups known as the twelve tribes of Israel. In this case, Israel is used to name the entire people group. What appears to be a count noun takes on aspects of a mass noun, as there is no way to know how many people comprise the tribes. The singular term is also used in a spatial sense to describe the land of the Northern Kingdom, as opposed to the southern kingdom of Judah.

Diagram 5.3 *Scoping out of the term Israel*

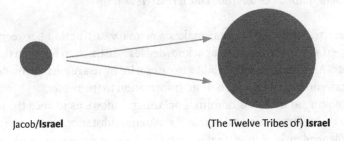

Jacob/**Israel**   (The Twelve Tribes of) **Israel**

As the illustration makes clear, there is a significant scoping of the referents for the term Israel in biblical usage, from human scale for the individual, to a much larger scale in the case of the term used for the entire group that lived in the Northern Kingdom. This scoping is also present in reverse in Jeremiah 2:14, which metaphorically summarizes the state of Israel's fortunes after the fall of Israel to the Assyrians, with the statement, "Is Israel a slave? Is he a homeborn servant? Why then has he become plunder?" (NRSV). In this case, the thought runs in the other direction, scoping the larger referent, Israel, to human scale, described as a slave or homeborn servant:

Diagram 5.4 *Scoping in of the term Israel*

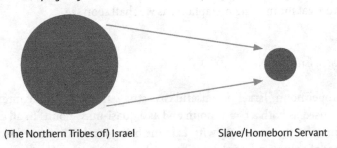

(The Northern Tribes of) Israel   Slave/Homeborn Servant

In this case, the writer has compressed all the people of Israel into terminology that is at human scale, which makes it easy to think about Israel's troublesome fall to the Assyrians.

In traditional grammar, verbs are typically described according to form. Students of biblical languages often spend considerable time with Greek and Hebrew verbal paradigms, learning forms and patterns—and then discover that there is almost always an exception to every grammatical rule. Alternatively, cognitive grammar looks at both form and function, including both the grammatical form and the semantics of a given statement. This differentiation between *lexicon* versus *usage event* reveals at least three distinct types of verbal processes: *event statements* describe activities. These generally include fully conjugated verbal forms. Sentences such as "Sarah laughed" and "Jesus wept" are event statements. *Relational statements* profile possessive and circumstantial situations. These often include verbless clauses, such as nouns in apposition, where a form of the verb "to be" is included in English translations. Jeremiah 2:14 includes two such clauses: "Is Israel a slave? Is he a homeborn servant?" There is no "is" in the original language text. Finally, *mental processes* include ideas such as thinking, seeing, hearing, knowing, believing, and so on. Sentences and phrases like "Jacob dreamed" and "I thought that you would return to me" give an insider view of the perceptions, thoughts, and beliefs of a character in the text. Verbs of speaking can also open the thoughts of a character, but also function to mark the narration. These categories are important for the discussion of Text World Theory in chapter 12.

Example 2: The Midwives

The story of the Hebrew midwives in Exodus 1:15–20 contains examples of each of these verbal categories: event statements, relational statements, and a single perception statement. In the text below, event statements are in bold, relational statements are underlined, and, for effect, verbs of speaking are in italics.

> [15]The king of Egypt *said* to the Hebrew midwives, one of whom was named Shiphrah and the other Puah, [16]"When you act as midwives to the Hebrew women, and see them on the birthstool, if it is a boy, kill him; but if it is a girl, she shall live." [17]But the midwives **feared** God; they did not do as the king of Egypt commanded them, but they let the boys live. [18]So the king of Egypt **summoned** the midwives and *said* to them, "Why have you done this, and allowed the boys to live?" [19]The midwives *said* to Pharaoh, "Because the Hebrew women are not like the Egyptian women; for they are vigorous and give birth before the midwife comes to them." [20]So God **dealt well** with the midwives; and the people multiplied and became very strong. (NRSV)

The conversation between the king of Egypt and the Hebrew midwives is presented as a series of event statements, including instances of speaking. The king of Egypt "said," the midwives "feared" God, the king of Egypt "summoned" the midwives and "said" to them, the midwives respond. Importantly, the statement "the midwives feared" participates both as an event statement and as a perception statement. Formally, the statement is part of the narrative string, while the perception verb itself reveals the midwives' internal disposition. The midwives' response contains two relational statements: "the Hebrew women are not like the Egyptian women; for they are vigorous." This delicious dig at the king is even more delightful because, as the reader realizes, they are lying. The two statements are stylistically significant, drawing attention to the contrast between the Hebrew women and the Egyptian women.

The playful term "little words" comprises relation words such as prepositions, adverbs, and particles that have little semantic content on their own but add a tremendous amount of meaning to the phrases in which they occur. Terms such as "in," "out," "on," "upon," "to," "toward," "under," and "unto" provide spatial information. Terms such as "I," "we," "you," "they," and "them" play into person deixis, and terms such as "here," "there," "now," and "then" give information related to a speaker or character in a text. When reading in translation, it is good to ascertain whether the spatial and temporal terms are individual words in the original language, or if the verb itself includes directionality in its semantic profile. For example, there are full verbs in Hebrew for "come in" and "go out" that do not contain a preposition.

Example 3: Little Words and Image Schemas

The beautiful imagery in Isaiah 40:11 invokes the CONTAINMENT SCHEMA via the repeated use of the preposition "in":

> He will feed his flock like a shepherd;
> he will gather the lambs *in* his arms,
> and carry them *in* his bosom,
> and gently lead the mother sheep. (NRSV)

The phrases evoke a nearly irresistible sense of safety for those being enfolded in strong arms, which form a boundary that separates the embraced from the outside world.

God's words to Moses in Exodus 3:10 also invoke the CONTAINMENT SCHEMA, this time using the preposition "out": "So come, I will send you to Pharaoh to bring my people, the Israelites, *out* of Egypt."

While a preponderance of the references to God leading the Israelites out of Egypt use the full verbal form of the verb "to lead out," in this case the preposition is used to talk about the highly significant beginning point of the exodus story. This sentence also invokes the SOURCE-PATH-GOAL SCHEMA, as Egypt is the initial point of the Israelites' movement from slavery to freedom—out of Egypt, into the desert, through the desert, out of the desert and into the promised land. Clearly, "little words" can invoke meaning far beyond their size.

Short History

The 1980s brought a rise in cognitive studies from a variety of perspectives. As part of this cognitive turn, Ronald Langacker revisited and reimagined grammar from a cognitive perspective, introducing the idea that speakers and writers were responsible for the way terms, clauses, and sentences are used and construed. Cognitive approaches have flourished over the decades and, while the body of work in cognitive linguistics, conceptual metaphor, and blending theory has grown exponentially, there are fewer studies that continue to focus solely on cognitive grammar. There are many studies that incorporate Langacker's seminal work in the broader cognitive linguistics frame, including William Croft and D. Alan Cruse, who include a section on construal in their volume, *Cognitive Linguistics* (2004). Additionally, David Lee has explained the cognitive grammar take on nouns and verbs at an accessible and useful level in his volume, *Cognitive Linguistics: An Introduction* (2001). Zoltán Kövecses provides a summary of construal in his chapter "Alternative Construals of the World" in *Language, Mind and Culture: A Practical Introduction* (Kövecses and Koller 2006) that allows readers to see the implications of various grammatical options for discussing a single event and what this means regarding culture. A recent and notable addition to the cognitive grammar fold is Giovanelli and Harrison's volume, *Cognitive Grammar in Stylistics* (2018), where they have abstracted key cognitive linguistics concepts in service of stylistics. *Cognitive Grammar in Stylistics* provides a lucid and applicable take on cognitive grammar and the reading process.

Related Features in Biblical Studies

Cognitive grammar taken on its own is a detailed and rather complicated discipline to bring to biblical studies, but as a part of cognitive linguistics and cognitive stylistics, it can provide tools for reading well, specifically in the areas of translation and interpretation. While this volume is aimed at reading modern translations well, the issue of translation comes up when multiple modern translations use different words to translate a single Hebrew word such as *hesed* or a Greek word such as *agapē*. The Hebrew word requires many English words to be fully understood (covenant love and faithfulness) and the Greek word in context can be construed in several ways (love of God, brotherly love, human love).

Translation of the biblical text is a vast area of research and practice. Various English translations have been the product of a large cadre of scholars working within theoretical frameworks that vary from adherence to a word-for-word model to those that are on a quest for dynamic equivalence, an idea-for-idea model. The understanding that grammar itself can be described in terms of usage events can help translators by allowing the translator to be on the lookout for constructions, analyzing whole phrases when moving from the source language to the target language. Translators can bear in mind individual lexical meanings for single words and look for how the words are related at the phrase or sentence level to form a whole idea, then look for similar relations in the target language.

Our main concern here is reading well as the primary step in biblical interpretation. Since biblical interpretation takes the text as a starting point, the issue of translation remains at the forefront. While word studies regarding individual words such as *hesed* and *agapē* are important for reading in translation, interpreters, like translators, can also examine the way that individual words are related to one another at the clause and sentence level. Online resources and Bible software bring a plethora of information to the table, even for those who do not have formal training in biblical languages. Such programs include formal analysis, and some include advanced linguistic analysis as well.

The Meaning of Cognitive Grammar in Biblical Studies

While cognitive grammar on its own is a bit technical and obscure, some of the principles of cognitive grammar, taken in conjunction with cognitive linguistics and cognitive stylistics, can add meaning for biblical studies. The main idea, that grammar is an embodied phenomenon, gives rise to the many ways that grammatical structures play on our understanding of the world around us. Seeing nouns as things and verbs as events reflects the way we perceive life in time and space. It helps us to grapple with statements such as "the earth was a formless void" in Genesis 1:2. In this statement, a nominal is not behaving in a typical, bounded way. Our sense of the earth as we know it is disrupted, creating forward motion for the narration.

Thus far we have looked at the proper noun, Israel, and have seen how a single nominal can be used to describe a single referent and how the same nominal can be used metaphorically to describe a far larger referent, comprised of many individuals, by scoping it to human scale. We have seen how the writer of Exodus used two verbless clauses to draw a powerful comparison between the Hebrew women and the Egyptian women—and then used the (likely false) idea to taunt the king. We have seen how the Isaiah text makes use of prepositional phrases, image schemas, and metaphor to comfort the exiles. Now let us look at a longer example and make some cognitive grammatical observations.

Case Study: Isaiah 2:1–4

Isaiah 2:1–4 is a prophetic oracle that contains several curious instances of language in use. While cognitive grammar tends to function at the word/clause/phrase levels, it is possible to work with a longer stretch of text as well. The text reads:

> [1] The word that Isaiah son of Amoz saw concerning Judah and Jerusalem.
> [2] In days to come
>   the mountain of the LORD's house
> shall be established as the highest of the mountains,
>   and shall be raised *above* the hills;
> all the nations shall stream *to* it.
>   [3] Many peoples shall come and say,
> "Come, let us go up to the mountain of the LORD,
>   to the house of the God of Jacob;
> that he may teach us his ways
>   and that we may walk *in* his paths."
> For *out* of Zion shall go forth instruction,
>   and the word of the LORD *from* Jerusalem.
>   [4] He shall judge *between* the nations,

> and shall arbitrate for many peoples;
> they shall beat their swords *into* <u>plowshares</u>,
> and their spears *into* <u>pruning hooks</u>;
> nation shall not lift up sword against nation,
> neither shall they learn war any more. (NRSV)

Looking at this text through the cognitive grammar lens invites several observations. First, some of the "things" involved in this stretch of text are slightly unusual: verse 1 discusses the word that Isaiah "saw." Normally we would expect to hear a word; however, Isaiah is known to have seen visions, which may prove to be a clue here. Secondly, there is the rather obscure reference to "the mountain of the LORD's house." Knowing that the temple was considered the "LORD's house" is a likely indication that this is what is being referred to, with the idea of a mountain giving emphasis to the idea of height. In fact, verse 2 indicates that the mountain shall be the highest point.

The SOURCE-PATH-GOAL IMAGE SCHEMA is particularly evident in the choice of individual verbs such as "go up" in verse 2 and in some of the verbs plus prepositional phrases marked in italics and underlining, such as "*out* of <u>Zion</u> shall go forth" in verse 3. There Zion is the source and the movement of instruction from there into the larger world is the path. Interestingly there is no defined goal. The term "Zion" itself evokes the CONTAINMENT SCHEMA when used in the phrase "out of Zion," a phenomenon it holds in common with the phrase "out of Egypt" discussed above. The repeated mention of height, mountain, and going up places the reader at the foot of the hill, awaiting the day when the height of the temple mount will be the dominant sight in Jerusalem. The aggregate of these observations points to the renewal of peace, something that has been elusive for the Israelites who had lost Temple and land to the Babylonians.

Ideas for Discussion

Here are a few ideas for further discussion, arranged alphabetically.

A is for Agony

In the introduction we discussed how the term "fight" is used in 1 Timothy 6:12 and how the reader uses clues in the text to work out the grammatical function of each instance. While the translated term is identical in the NRSV English translation, the meaning is disambiguated by looking at the original Greek text, where the first usage is clearly a verb and the second is clearly a noun. The intersection of form and function is further affected by the translation process because choices made by the translators may also affect the reader's understanding of the term.

1. Read 1 Timothy 6:12 in several English translations. (An online source such as BlueLetterBible.org can be helpful for finding a variety of versions.)
2. What other English words are used for the verbal idea, "fight"?
3. What other English words are used for the noun idea, "fight"?
4. In what ways do these choices affect your understanding of the sentence?
5. Both Greek terms are found in the Louw-Nida Dictionary under section 39.29, which includes the short definition, "to struggle, to fight." In what ways do the translations soften or reinforce this short definition?

B is for Baby (Jesus)

Image schemas often structure sections of biblical text and paying attention to them can help the reader to track through the text. The story of Jesus's birth is one such section.

1. Read the story of Jesus's birth in Luke 2:1-20.
2. Look for examples of the SOURCE-PATH-GOAL SCHEMA, marked by event statements that include terms such as "go" or "went."
3. Name the source and goal points. Are they indicated by time reference, spatial reference, or something else? For example, look for where Joseph started and ended his journey in verse 4 and compare it with the source and goal points for the shepherds' journey in verses 8-16. How about the source and goal points for the angel in verses 9-15?
4. How do these journeys help you to visualize the background of the birth of baby Jesus?

Further Reading

For the seminal treatment of cognitive grammar, see Ronald W. Langacker, *Foundations of Cognitive Grammar* (1983), and Ronald W. Langacker, *Foun-*

dations of Cognitive Grammar, vol. 1 (1987). These volumes provide both the extended theory and the descriptive application for cognitive grammar. They are for the intrepid reader, who will doubtless gain much, but likely at the cost of time and effort.

For those on a focussed, but less intense quest, a more accessible treatment of cognitive grammar may be found in Ronald W. Langacker, *Grammar and Conceptualization* (1999); Ronald W. Langacker, "Discourse in Cognitive Grammar" (2001); and most specifically Ronald W. Langacker, *Concept, Image, and Symbol: The Cognitive Basis of Grammar* (2002). Finally, David Lee provides an exceptionally accessible and useful presentation of cognitive grammar in his volume, *Cognitive Linguistics: An Introduction* (2001).

Application-oriented pieces include Langacker's essay, "Context, Cognition, and Semantics: A Unified Dynamic Approach" (2003), and Hayes's volume, *The Pragmatics of Perception and Cognition in MT Jeremiah 1:1–6:30: A Cognitive Linguistics Approach* (2008). In this volume Hayes incorporates several cognitive grammar insights into a cognitive linguistics based theory for text analysis at levels higher than the sentence. Also see Zoltán Kövecses and Bálint Koller, *Language, Mind, and Culture: A Practical Introduction* (2006).

For an exceptionally productive application of cognitive grammar as it relates to stylistics, see Marcello Giovanelli and Chloe Harrison, *Cognitive Grammar in Stylistics: A Practical Guide* (2018).

Mapping Corresponding Dots

What Comes Next

The Predictability of Schemas and Scripts

And the Story Goes

The exodus forms one of the key passages of the Bible. After a period of oppression, God leads his people out of Egypt under the guidance of Moses. The journey does not go smoothly: Moses initially thinks he is not fit for the task, Pharaoh repeatedly refuses to let the people go, and when the people finally leave, they run into the Red Sea. Fortunately, this water miraculously parts for the Israelites so that they can continue their return home. The journey goes through the desert, where they lack food and water, which God eventually provides. Other books of the Bible, both in the Old and New Testament, pick up the event of the exodus. With a few simple words, Isaiah and Paul bring back the experience of oppression and consequent delivery.

All about Scripts and Schemas

As you started reading the above introduction, you thought of the exodus, the Israelites' journey out of Egypt. You imagined a starting point to be left and a destination to be reached. Perhaps you also thought of the movie *Exodus: Gods and Kings* (2014), which is based on the biblical event. Or you imagined the exodus more generally as a movement of people out of a place, for example, the exodus of Africans to Europe or the exodus of educated South-Europeans to Northern Europe or the US. In other words, you were drawing on a kind of scenario in your mind to understand the specific exodus mentioned in the biblical text. Scholars call such a scenario a **schema**. A schema is a larger knowledge structure that is more or less stable but dynamic, meaning that our experiences will further refine it. Thus, we have an idea of what an exodus is, but viewing the movie mentioned or following the news on migration will change the specifics of the schema. A schema is a structured bit of context or background knowledge a reader relies on and that is triggered by the text. This means that a schema is an interaction between elements in the text (what scholars describe as **projection** or a **bottom-up process**) and pre-existing knowledge brought by the reader to the text (called **construction** or a **top-down process**). Reading a text is combining these two processes (see diagram 6.1).

Diagram 6.1 *Schema production*

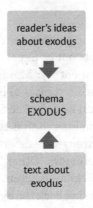

For example, when God addresses Moses in Exodus 3, he mentions "the affliction of his people" and "their outcry" and "oppressors." These words in the text trigger an OPPRESSION schema or even a SLAVERY schema for the reader. This is further affirmed by what follows: God's plan to rescue his people and bring them home. It also evokes a second schema, that of DELIVERANCE, cued by words such as "rescue" and "bring out." The specific words are part of the bottom-up process; they are the text speaking to the reader. Simultaneously, the reader will speak to the text, when completing the schema evoked by the words. Readers have previous knowledge about oppression and deliverance. They know that the former is a bad experience, involving a lack of freedom, physical and/or mental abuse, a hierarchy in which one party has significantly more power than the other, and so on. The latter, the DELIVERANCE schema, includes a savior, someone to be rescued, feelings of gratitude and happiness, an improvement of the situation, and so on.

Diagram 6.2 *Construction of OPPRESSION schema*

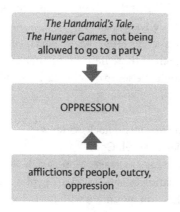

Whereas the text itself only mentions a few elements to activate a particular schema, our mind will fill in the missing information, based on our previous experiences with oppression and deliverance, respectively. Note that experience does not stand for personal experience per se. Having seen, heard, or read about oppression or deliverance is enough to build up background knowledge that will be used when reading Exodus 3. Thus, a contemporary American reader will have a schema of oppression that is influenced by books such as *The Handmaid's Tale* and films such as *The Hunger Games* series. One's own personal experience with oppression may be limited to that one time they wanted to go to a party but were not allowed to (see diagram 6.2).

Scholars use small capital letters for the names of schemas, an annotation they use for all knowledge structures. As we will see later, also **conceptual metaphors** and **metonymies** will be referred to using small capital letters. All of them are examples of the **Idealized Cognitive Models** or **ICMs** mentioned earlier in the chapter on prototypes.

Models such as schemas are triggered by cues in the text, called *headers*. There are four types of them: precondition headers, instrumental headers, locale headers, and internal conceptualization headers. Think, as an example, of the passage in which God calls Moses (opening of Exodus 3). The active schema is that of a SPEECH. A *precondition header* is that God has something to say and Moses is able to listen. These elements create the circumstances for the speech. *Instrumental headers* are actions that lead to the realization of the schema, such as, the burning bush drawing Moses's attention. Schemas have a specific setting, evoked by *locale headers*. Moses is on mount Horeb when

God speaks to him. Finally, *internal conceptualization headers* have to do with actions or roles that are typical of the schema. A speech requires a speaker and a listener, a message to be delivered, etc.

Headers refer to *slots*, such as *props, participants, entry conditions, results,* and *sequence of events*. Each of these helps to further categorize the information in the text and entangle the setup of schemas. Consider the list below for the example of Moses's call in Exodus 3.

props	burning bush, flock, sandals
participants	Moses, angel, God
entry conditions	need for a message, Moses available for listening
results	situation of oppression in Egypt will be taken care of
sequence of events	Moses on mountain with flock–burning bush–call Moses by name–Moses ready to listen–deliver message

Thus far, we have addressed what schemas are. The next step is to consider what they mean for reading. Schemas are about *predictability* and *reader expectations*. When we read that the angel is calling out to Moses, we expect a speech to be delivered afterward. When we learn about the Israelites' oppression, we anticipate a DELIVERANCE schema to end this oppression. Scholars will speak of a *schema preservation* or *reinforcement* when the expectations of readers are confirmed by the text. Thus, in this case a speech is given and the people are freed. The schema we had identified based on the textual headers as well as our previous experience with it appears to be used further on in the story. Schema preservation is our basic expectation, our starting point: we assume that the world in the text will function in a way similar to the world we know. This is called the *principle of minimal departure*. We expect that the textual headers will match our pre-existing knowledge, resulting in a coherent schema.

However, texts and writers do more than affirm. They also purposefully play and challenge existing schemas. When God asks Moses to be his spokesman, Moses says no. This does not fit our DELIVERANCE schema. If Moses does not fulfill this role, the schema lacks a deliverer. It is a *schema disruption*. Yet, the story continues, and God suggests Aaron could do the talking, without acquitting Moses. At that point, the DELIVERANCE schema undergoes a *refreshment*. Deliverance will be achieved by means of two helpers instead of one. Moses's initial "no" becomes a "yes, but." One could also call this a *schema accretion* in which new elements are added, here Aaron.

Diagram 6.3 *Schema disruption and schema refreshment*

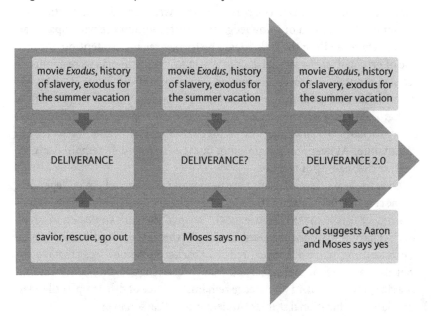

Schemas do not only play a role in terms of content (called *world schemas*), but there are also text and language schemas. The DELIVERANCE schema is an example of a world schema, but this comes with a *text schema*, such as a narrative, a song (the song of the sea), dialogue, and their specific structural organization. *Language schemas* are about the appropriate style and linguistic setup, such as poetry for a prophecy or turn-taking in a dialogue. When God calls Moses in Exodus 3, the text schema is a CALL NARRATIVE. This typically includes a divine being addressing a human being, either personally or through a messenger. Furthermore, it often comes with supernatural signs, such as a burning bush, and happens unexpectantly as far as the receiver goes (Moses is shepherding the flock). In a CALL NARRATIVE, the caller is the primary speaker, with minor interruptions by the addressee. Language schemas for such a narrative are second-person address and the use of imperatives or cohortative forms.

Short History

The psychologist Frederic C. Bartlett developed schema theory in the 1930s in a study on how people remember folk tales. He discovered that people replaced unfamiliar information with more familiar information. They also added new elements in the retellings. The reason for this was, according to Bartlett, the existence of schemata or knowledge structures, which the participants accessed when retelling the folk tales. The theory regained attention with the rise of *artificial intelligence (AI)* after World War II. Schemas were applied to assist computers in processing human language and thinking. Scholars had noticed that understanding even a simple phrase requires a huge amount of background knowledge. Schemas provided computer programs with this necessary *background knowledge*, also called context (Schank and Abelson 1977). Meanwhile, AI keeps on progressing, but the first models remain useful to analyze the reading of texts.

Over the years, several terms have been used to refer to schemas, depending on the research field as well as the specific emphasis placed. These terms include "frames" (Minsky 1975; Fillmore 1985), "scripts" (Schank and Abelson 1977), and "scenarios" (Sanford and Garrod 1981). All these labels fundamentally have the same thing in mind: a structured bit of background knowledge that readers (but also speakers, of course) rely on when processing a text (or conversation). The size of this chunk of knowledge remains an issue of debate up until today, especially in educational studies (Anderson and Pearson 1984).

Related Features in Biblical Studies

One of the big issues in biblical studies is context. What was the context of the original text and how does the context of later readers influence the interpretation of the text? The study of the biblical text nowadays typically involves learning more about the background of the text, in other words, reconstructing the schemas that the original audience could tap into without an effort. Traditionally, scholarship pays attention to the historical interpretation of context—When was the text written? Under which circumstances? By whom? What were the social and political circumstances? and so on. Schemas and scripts address this difficult notion of context from a different angle. Rather than saying that the Last Supper is set in ancient Palestine, near the Mount of Olives, probably around the year 0 of the common era, the context would be the schema of a SUPPER. You have people who invite and prepare the meal, and people who are guests. There is typically food and drinks. In addition to eating and drinking, people also tend to talk and share experiences over the meal. Those gathering at one's home are friends, and so on. Note that the SUPPER schema of the gospel does not differ greatly in its basic setup from the current-day SUPPER schema. As will be shown below under "Further Study," such is not always the case, resulting in schema disruption.

Two other topics that draw implicitly on schema theory come from the narratological study of the biblical text: the concept of type-scenes and the notion of gaps in the text. In his study of biblical narrative, Robert Alter introduced the idea of type-scenes (1980), which itself came from the broader literary field, particularly from the study of Homer's works. Type-scenes are scenes that draw on a specific set of actions, participants, and objects. Alter uses Rebekah's betrothal scene in Genesis 24 as an example. All other betrothal scenes showcase the same set of actions, participants, and objects, so that these scenes also can be recognized as betrothal scenes. In schema theory words, Genesis 24 uses a BETROTHAL schema. Readers pick up the cues in the text and anticipate what is coming based on their knowledge of the BETROTHAL schema. Type-scenes would fall under the category of schema preservation or reinforcement. They affirm what people expect.

Another narratological feature that draws on schema theory is that of gaps in the text (Sternberg 1985). One of the key characteristics of biblical narrative is its succinct writing style. Rather than providing the reader with long-winding descriptions and an abundance of details, the text contains various gaps. Some of these gaps are simply part of schemas that modern readers either do not know anymore or do not dare to fill in because of the sacred status of the text. For example, the binding of Isaac (Gen. 22) does not tell us about Sarah or Isaac's feelings, true, but schema theory acknowledges the actual role and presence of each of the characters in the story. The schema of SACRIFICE requires participants, such as someone who sacrifices, someone to whom is sacrificed, and something or someone to be sacrificed. One would set out on a journey to the place to sacrifice, saying your goodbyes to those left behind (which is where Sarah comes into the schema). Once the sacrifice is over, the person would return with all those that were initially with him (which means also with Isaac since he was not sacrificed after all). If SACRIFICE is the dominant schema in Genesis 22, it makes sense that the text does not focus on the relations between Sarah and Abraham or Sarah and Isaac, which would be part of a FAMILY schema. Genesis 22 foregrounds the SACRIFICE schema. The reason why modern-day readers ask questions about Sarah and Isaac partially has to do with the fact that in our day and age the FAMILY schema at least competes with or is even more important than a SACRIFICE schema. What is more, our FAMILY schema is also fundamentally different from that of the text. Husband and wife are equal partners, who discuss important things with each other. In addition, violence of any form in a FAMILY schema is evaluated negatively.

This is not to say that the Bible's gaps are always to be filled in with schema knowledge. Yet, schemas do help us to understand how gaps are not always gaps and how different schemas of different audiences and their prioritizing of one over the other play into that.

The Meaning of Scripts and Schemas in Biblical Studies

Schemas are an excellent tool to address the notion of context and background knowledge in biblical studies. They bring together other approaches to context such as historical, literary, or reader-based ones (e.g., in feminist or postcolonial studies). For example, when the people complain to Moses in the desert, a reader will draw on a HARDSHIP schema to understand the text. Cues in the text point the reader in this direction: the people lack water and food, the journey is exceptionally long, the promised land is far away, and so on. These are bottom-up aspects a literary approach would typically point out. A historical approach will consider the environmental circumstances as well as the circumstances of travel in antiquity. This is top-down information added to the understanding of the text. In addition, a reader may have been in the desert themselves or may have experienced an extremely hot summer day where they forgot their water bottle at home. This is another top-down piece of knowledge that informs the HARDSHIP schema. Thus, schemas are not simplifications of the stories, but, on the contrary, draw on various views on the text that all inform the eventual understanding of this text.

Schemas are particularly helpful to assess different interpretations of a text. The history of biblical interpretation provides plentiful illustrations. For example, is the Song of Songs love poetry? Or rather an allegory for the relationship between God and the church? Or perhaps it is an invective directed to Solomon? Each of these interpretations uses a different schema to read the Song of Songs. Signals in the text as well as pre-existing knowledge of the reader bring reader A to a LOVE POEM schema, reader B to an ALLEGORY schema and reader C to an INVECTIVE schema. Schemas are reader dependent, hence the different interpretations. Nevertheless, all the suggested interpretations rely on elements present in the text.

Via schemas readers also get insight into how typical story elements, such as surprise or humor, work. Both of these elements function as schema disruptions. For example, consider the following words of Jesus: "Why do you see the speck in your brother's eye, but do not perceive the beam in your own eye? How can you say to your brother, 'Let me remove the speck from your eye,' while the beam is in your eye?" (Matt. 7:3–4).[1] The structure of the sentence sets readers up for an **analogy** (a LANGUAGE schema). If A is similar to B and A is true, so B must be true. However, Matthew disrupts the pattern, leaving the reader wondering. What is more, readers will also expect practical, and thus literal, guidelines from Jesus, as they appear in verses 1 and 2 of the chapter (TEXT schema). Again, this is schema disruption, which some would interpret as surprise, others even as humor. The reader did not see that beam coming; however, they will surely remember. Likewise, the idea of a whole plank in one's eye seems a little outrageous. Readers may not laugh out loud, but they may smile at least by the thought of it. In real life, it is very unlikely indeed that one would not notice a beam in one's eye, let alone bother in that case about the splinter in someone else's eye (WORLD schema disruption).

When it comes to the biblical text, another element forms an excellent topic of a schema approach: *ideology*. The Bible presents very specific ideas on the divine, worship, community, piety, sin, and so on. For example, a schema we find throughout the text is that of SIN AND REPENTANCE. By tracking this schema in different stories, we can identify passages where the schema is reinforced and where it is disrupted. In the end, following the Bible's ideological schemas helps us understand which schemas are important for the Bible and what is done with them. As with all previous examples, such an analysis includes taking into account a reader's pre-existing knowledge about these schemas and this knowledge's influence on the schema we build up based on textual cues.

Case Study: The Ten Plagues

Schemas clarify the story of the ten plagues of Egypt (Exod. 7–12). Let us consider the first plague in Exodus 7 as an illustration. Upon God's request, Moses and Aaron have a conversation with Pharaoh, but without result. Pharaoh does not let the Israelites go. This is when God introduces the first plague.

> [14] And the LORD said to Moses, "Pharaoh's heart is *stubborn*; he *refuses* to let the people go. [15] Go to Pharaoh in the morning, as he is going out to the water, and stand on the bank of the Nile to meet him, taking in your hand the staff that turned into a serpent. [16] And you will say to him, 'The LORD, the God of the Hebrews, sent me to you to say, "Let my people go that they

---

1. All translations in this chapter are the author's own.

may worship me in the wilderness." But you have not listened until now.
¹⁷ Thus says the LORD, "By this you shall know that I am the LORD." Behold,
I will strike the water in the Nile with the rod that is in my hand, and it
will turn into blood. ¹⁸ And the fish in the Nile will die and the Nile will
stink, and the Egyptians will grow weary of drinking water from the Nile.'"
    ²³ And Pharaoh turned and went into his house, and he did not take
even this to heart.

In verse 14, the reader comes across a stubborn Pharaoh who refuses to
let the people go, even though he was asked nicely. In other words, we have a
divine command disobeyed. This evokes a schema of DISCIPLINE or PUNISH-
MENT. The text does not need to be as specific as saying: Pharaoh did wrong,
so God is going to punish him, whereupon he will say sorry and do as asked
eventually. Rather, as readers, we connect the cues in the text with our background knowledge of transgressors and evildoers. We remember that time we
drove too fast and got a speeding ticket, or Bart Simpson being grounded for
telling a lie to his mom. The schema is further constructed with information
from the text: the edge of the Nile is a locale header; God's request and Pharaoh's disobedience to it function as precondition headers; and the setup of
two parties (God and Pharaoh), a broken rule (let them go) and a punishment
(blood Nile) form *conceptualization* headers.

As we go through the story of the first plague, our DISCIPLINE schema is
preserved. Pharaoh is indeed punished. However, at two points, we as readers
may be surprised. For one, God punishes not only Pharaoh but all the Egyptians with him. If our schema assumes that only the evildoer is disciplined,
we can consider this a schema disruption. However, we can *downgrade* this
disruption, that is, offer an explanation that allows us to integrate it in the
existing schema, nevertheless. For example, ancient societies place the community over the individual. Hence, if one person sins, the whole community
is punished. Or, as a leader Pharaoh represents the whole nation. If he sins,
everyone is affected. Or, the punishment has a rhetorical function: it is used
to convince Pharaoh by greatly overcompensating the sin. A second surprise
comes at the end of the first plague. Despite God's intervention, Pharaoh does
not listen. The punishment does not work. If we keep on reading, we will see
that the plague narratives refresh our DISCIPLINE schema. Rather than the
punishment being effective, Pharaoh continues to be stubborn. Thus, the book
of Exodus develops its very own version of the DISCIPLINE schema, in which
only after the tenth plague does Pharaoh give in long enough for the Israelites
to escape Egypt. The first "no" of Pharaoh surprises the reader, the final "yes"

does as well. Through a play with schemas the writers have created a tale that keeps the reader engaged until the very end.

What is more, paying attention to schemas activated during reading allows explaining as well as discussing different interpretations of the first plague. A theological interpretation of the passage does not question the nature of the punishment. A blood Nile is as real as a slap in the face. However, readers who understand the blood Nile as a natural phenomenon will consider the punishment a schema disruption. If the red color of the Nile is a natural phenomenon caused by debris and algae during the flood season, God's main intervention has to do with timing rather than with a powerful reprimand. This short example shows that schemas are worth considering when dealing with interpreting biblical texts. What is more, they play as much a role in our own interpretation as in that of all those who have studied the text before us.

Ideas for Discussion

1. Schemas help us to navigate a text. They prepare us for what is coming (or not, if the schema is disrupted). Consider the following two texts, the story of Ehud and Eglon in Judges 3:12–30 and the story of the empty grave in John 20:1-18. Which schemas can you identify in each of them? Can you point out headers in the text? Which additional information from your personal experience did you add to the schemas?
2. Compare your schemas from the previous exercise with that of your neighbor. To what extent do they differ? Can you explain the differences?
3. Characters in the Bible are often described as flat, meaning that they evolve little to nothing. How would you assess this observation applying schema theory? And how would this use of characters fit the larger framework of the Bible as an ideological document? Consider the figure of Abraham (Old Testament) or Peter (New Testament). Which schema do they fit? Where do you come across schema disruptions, reinforcements, or accretions in their respective stories?
4. Read the following text passage. Where can you detect schemas, headers?

> [1] Ah city of blood,
>   full of lies and plunder
>   where killing never stops!
> [2] Crack of whip and rattle of wheel,
>   galloping steed and bounding chariot!
> [3] Charging horsemen,

> flashing swords, and glittering spears!
> A multitude of slain and
> heaps of corpses,
> there is no end to dead bodies,
> they stumble over bodies.
> [4] Because of the many harlotries of the harlot,
> the charming mistress of sorcery,
> who sells nations by her harlotries
> and peoples by her sorcery,
> [5] I am going to deal with you—
> declares the LORD of hosts.
> I will lift your skirts over your face
> and I will show your nakedness to nations
> and your shame to kingdoms.

5. The previous passage comes from the book of Nahum, chapter 3. This book contains a prophecy against Nineveh, in which, contrary to Jonah's tale, there is no room for repentance. The city will be destroyed. Nineveh is personified in a way similar to Jerusalem and also Babylon in other prophetic books. With this additional information in mind, reread the passage and redraw your schema. Would you stick to the same schema, or would you consider a different one? What eventual changes did you make to your initial schema?
6. Think of a biblical text that you have read many times under different circumstances. How did your understanding of that text evolve? Was your schema reinforced, disrupted, or accredited?

Further Reading

Accessible introductions of schema theory for reading texts appear in Guy Cook, *Discourse and Literature: The Interplay of Form and Mind* (1994); Elena Semino, *Language and World Creation in Poems and Other Texts* (1997, 119–94); Peter Stockwell, *Cognitive Poetics: An Introduction* (2002, 75–90); Lesley Jeffries and Dan McIntyre, *Stylistics* (2010, 127–33); and Alison Gibbons and Sarah Whiteley, *Contemporary Stylistics: Language, Cognition, Interpretation* (2018, 175–82).

The basis for schema theory was led by Frederic C. Bartlett in his work *Remembering: A Study in Experimental and Social Psychology* (1932, reprint 1995). The following works discuss its further development in artificial intelligence: Roger C. Schank and Robert Abelson, *Scripts, Plans, Goals and Understanding* (1977), and Roger C. Schank, *Reading and Understanding: Teaching from the Perspective of Artificial Intelligence* (1982). More on frames can be found in Marvin Minsky, "A Framework for Representing Knowledge" (1975); Marvin Minsky, *The Society of Mind* (1986); and Charles Fillmore, "Frames and the Semantics of Understanding" (1985). Anthony J. Sanford and Simon C. Garrod write on scenarios in *Understanding Written Language* (1981). An example of schema theory in educational sciences is Richard C. Anderson and P. David Pearson, "A Schema-Theoretic View of Basic Processes in Reading Comprehension" (1984).

Various introductory works to the Bible as a whole or to specific books offer the reader background knowledge of different kinds. Two good examples are *The Hebrew Bible: A Critical Companion* (Barton 2016) and *An Introduction to the New Testament: The Abridged Edition* (Brown and Soards 2016). Chapter 3 of Robert Alter's well-known *The Art of Biblical Narrative* (1980) addresses type-scenes. Meir Sternberg discusses gaps in the biblical text in his *The Poetics of Biblical Narrative: Ideological Literature and the Drama of Reading* (1985, 186–229).

More insights on the plague narrative are offered by Greta Hort, "The Plagues of Egypt" (1959); Benedikte Lemmelijn, "Not Fact, Yet True: Historicity versus Theology in the 'Plague Narrative' (Ex 7–11)" (2007); and Siro Trevisanato, *The Plagues of Egypt: Archaeology, History and Science Look at the Bible* (2005).

Schemas applied to characters can be found in Jonathan Culpeper, *Language and Characterisation: People in Plays and Other Texts* (2001). Chloe Harrison and Louise Nuttall have studied the impact of rereading on schemas in "Re-reading in Stylistics" (2018).

SEVEN

How We See the Text

Mental Spaces and Blends

Thinking about Thinking

Mental Spaces Theory provides a fascinating look into how we process information and make meaning as we think and talk—and read. Conceptual blending makes use of mental spaces and offers additional insight into how we process information and make meaning as well. In this chapter we will look at the basics of Mental Spaces Theory and at the way that conceptual blending gives insight into how we combine information found in the text with information found in long-term memory to make meaning as we are reading the Bible. While Mental Spaces Theory is schematic in nature, dealing with how small information packets, called mental spaces, are formed, structured, and linked, conceptual blending builds on mental spaces insights, producing a fuller and more detailed understanding of how meaning is created.

All about Mental Spaces and Reading

An important aspect of the mental spaces discussion is that mental spaces are, for lack of a better description, "all in your head." Mental spaces are an online phenomenon—they operate while we think and talk. They function in our working memory and they also draw upon our long-term memory—that encyclopedic knowledge of the world that is also "all in our heads." They are set up, structured, and linked together as we think and talk and read. Mental spaces are cued and constrained by grammar, context, and culture. The text itself might prompt for new mental spaces when the author uses verbs of perception, cognition, and speech.

Language, Context, and Culture in Genesis 1

Mental spaces cued by the text are abundantly visible in the creation story in Genesis 1, which contains the repeated refrain, "Then/And God said" in verses 3, 6, 9, 11, 14, 20, 24, and 26. In verse 3, God said "Let there be light," and consequently, there was light. At the word "said," our attention is drawn away from the formless void and the wind sweeping across the waters and is focused on the voice of God—the verb "said" opens a new mental space that is structured by God's words. Verse 4 contains the evaluative statement, "And God saw." In this case, a verb of perception is used to describe what God thought about the light he created—the assessment is that, from God's perspective, it was good. With this statement, we are briefly invited into God's thoughts. (Well, into *one* of God's thoughts, leaving the rest of them unsaid.) This pattern of speaking and creating is repeated seven more times in the immediate context and God speaks and blesses three additional times in the same context (see vv. 22, 28, and 29). The mental spaces are linked by the identity of the speaker and by the repetition of the verb of speaking. The spaces continue to form as we read the text, forming a network of spaces that provide understanding about God's speaking role in the creation of the world and its creatures. This text is the product of an ancient culture, yet it speaks clearly to today's reader because we are familiar with how verbs of speaking partition language and how repetition can link ideas.

Other grammatical constructions can also act as space builders: prepositions can be used to shift attention in time and space, adverbs, conjunctions plus phrases, and so forth. This speaks to the way that conceptualization is a matter of both form and function.

Conceptual Blending and Reading the Bible

While mental spaces opened by verbs of speaking are very evident in Genesis 1, another conceptual operation occurs as we think and talk about creation in this chapter. Conceptual blending is active in how we form our ideas about a deity who speaks, acts, and evaluates the results of his activity. While some might say that a deity who speaks and evaluates is an example of **personification** (describing a nonhuman entity by using human traits), that definition does not fit the situation in the Genesis 1 text very well. God is present in Genesis 1:1, but God's creation of humankind takes place in Genesis 1:26-27. This leaves open the possibility that communicating and evaluating are things humans come by because they are created in the image of God, because they bear the *imago dei*, at least regarding this text. A conceptual blending diagram is helpful to sort out how we are thinking about these shared traits.

Thinking about God in Genesis 1 includes thinking about the idea that God speaks, perceives, and evaluates. Since these are activities typically associated with embodied humans, conceptual blending occurs as we read the text and try to make sense of a deity who is reported to do the same. Conceptual blending is a cognitive process that occurs as we think and talk, and it is another way that mental spaces are structured and linked to produce meaning. When reading the Genesis 1 account, the description of God and his creative activities precedes the creation of humankind, so one way to see this passage is to understand that communication, perception, and cognition are aspects of God's own self that are then reflected in created humankind as part of the *imago dei* mentioned in Genesis 1:27. Let us look at a way to account for the conceptual blending process represented by this text.

First, let us look at a basic conceptual blending diagram. A basic diagram is composed of four circles, or spaces. The topmost space contains information that is schematic and common to all the spaces. The two middle spaces are input spaces, and information that is common to these is connected via cross space mapping. Finally, selected information from the input spaces is represented in the blended space.

Diagram 7.1 *Simple conceptual blending diagram*

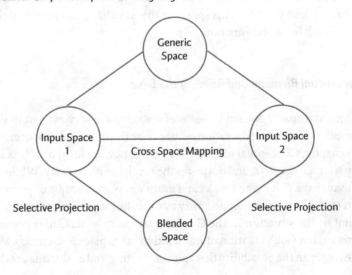

Now, let us fill in the basic diagram with information from the text of Genesis 1. The generic space contains the term "relationality," a broad term that indicates the common features of the information in the other three spaces. Input 1 contains the details about God we can glean from the text—God speaks, God sees, and God evaluates. Input 2 contains information about humankind that, while not explicit in the text, may be retrieved from our encyclopedic knowledge—as embodied beings, humans speak, humans see, and humans evaluate. From the text, we add the understanding that humankind is created in God's image. Finally, the blended space contains selected information common to both input 1 and input 2—the qualities of speech, perception, and cognition. From this blend, it becomes clear that these qualities are shared by humankind and the divine. Additionally, the quality of being created in God's image is attributed to humankind from the start. It seems that the shared qualities of speech, perception, and cognition are somehow connected to the *imago dei*, although the mystery of how these embodied qualities are associated with the God who creates remains.

Diagram 7.2 *The* imago dei: *conceptual blending for God and humankind in Genesis 1*

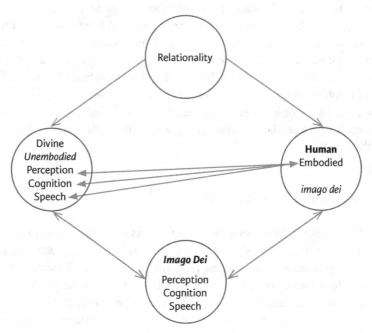

The various spaces in these diagrams are examples of the now familiar small knowledge packets known as mental spaces. However, the space building process in this instance is undertaken by analyzing sections of text larger than a sentence. This process comes into its fullness in Text World Theory, the subject of chapter 12.

Short History

Mental Spaces Theory and conceptual blending are aspects of the cognitive turn that began in the late 1980s and early 1990s. Gilles Fauconnier was curious about meaning construction in everyday language and worked to formulate a way to account for the cognitive operations present as we think and talk. This view of language sees the text as one part of the reading process and the mental aspects that underlie the reading as another, connected part. In this understanding, meaning is made as mental spaces are created, structured, and linked during language use.

In his theoretical discussions, Fauconnier described mappings such as those involved in processing counterfactuals, analogy, and metaphor (Fauconnier 1994, 1997). Fauconnier and Eve Sweetser gathered the work of several cognitive linguists who had begun working in the same area in their volume *Spaces, Worlds, and Grammar* (1996). Fauconnier also worked extensively with Mark Turner on blending theory, producing several articles and the very readable volume *The Way We Think: Conceptual Blending and the Mind's Hidden Complexities* (Fauconnier and Turner 2002). The idea of language and meaning as an embodied phenomenon found a voice in the work of linguists such as Mark Johnson (1987) and psychologists such as Raymond Gibbs (2006).

Related Features in Biblical Studies

The field of biblical studies is largely a text-based field and interpreters often engage with some version of a "close reading" when approaching a text. These careful readers observe the text and make note of characterization, genre, literariness, style, literary features, and issues of language, among other things. While many interpreters have studied the text at the sentence level, there has also been a trend in technical biblical studies to work with larger sections of text. This has taken several forms, from the literary approaches of Robert Alter and Meir Sternberg, to linguistic approaches to discourse analysis. The linguistic approaches often include detailed analysis of verbal forms and the creation of structural diagrams based on linguistic and grammatical forms.

The Meaning of Mental Spaces and Blends in Biblical Studies

Perhaps the most important aspect of Mental Spaces Theory for biblical studies is the idea that meaning is created in the process of reading and talking. The author and reader share a common text; however, the reader comes to the text many centuries after it was written. This has two main implications. First, some of the most effective connections are those that incorporate embodied notions, such as image schemas and other information that we share simply because we are embodied humans. Second, the state of the reader's encyclopedic background knowledge also comes into play: not every reader comes to the text with similar life experience or similar presuppositions. The injunction to "know thyself" remains apt. The more aware a reader is about their own background knowledge, the more accurately they will be able to discern the edges where presuppositions meet text. Conceptual blending occurs constantly as we think and talk and this is also reflected in the biblical text: rewritten Bible, literary features, genre, and more all recruit and combine information from various conceptual domains. Being observant of novel blends can add new information for reader and interpreter alike.

Case Study: Mental Spaces and Conceptual Blending in 2 Corinthians 6:14–18

The idea of a God who speaks, perceives, and evaluates is present throughout both the Old Testament and the New Testament. In fact, the reuse of Old Testament text in other parts of the Old Testament and in the New Testament is a fascinating area of study in and of itself, particularly when passages contain the idea of a speaking deity. It is even more interesting to consider the many shifts in context that have taken place as sections of the Old Testament have been learned, studied, and rewritten into the New Testament. Regarding the New Testament, scholars differentiate between explicit, or direct quotations that have a formal correspondence with previously written texts, and allusions, or echoes that are informal representations of a text that the author could pull from memory. Some talk about "rewritten Bible," a term that helps us to understand that there are layers of authorship involved, thus layers of contextual meaning. Before looking at mental space construction and blending in this text, an initial observation about cognitive connections is in order, as direct quotations and allusions provide two different sets of cognitive connections. Direct quotations provide *cross-text connections*, connecting one text to another, while allusions, or echoes, connect information between *author-text* spaces. In other words, allusions and echoes connect to the author's background knowledge, whereas quotations connect one text to another without invoking any more than authorial choice. That such quotations or allusions are used in a text says something about the author's view of the authority of Scripture: at minimum, Scripture is not just any text. This is made quite clear in 2 Corinthians 6:14-18.

In his Second Letter to the Corinthians, Paul sets forth many instructions for good and right living. His sometimes-convoluted arguments incorporate many direct quotations and allusions taken from the Old Testament text. Paul's reliance on Scripture demonstrates his respect for and dependence on what has been written before his time. In fact, the Scripture of his day was what we now call the Old Testament and that alone can account for his wide-ranging understanding and recounting of the Old Testament text in his arguments.

The NRSV of 2 Corinthians 6:14-18 reads:

[14] Do not be mismatched with unbelievers. For what partnership is there between righteousness and lawlessness? Or what fellowship is there between light and darkness? [15] What agreement does Christ have with Beliar? Or what does a believer share with an unbeliever? [16] What agreement has the temple of God with idols? For we are the temple of the living God; as **God said**,

> "I will live in them and walk among them,
>   and I will be their God,
>   and they shall be my people. [See Lev. 26:12.]
> [17] Therefore come out from them,
>   and be separate from them, **says the Lord**,
>   and touch nothing unclean; [See Isa. 52:11.]

then I will welcome you,
[18] and I will be your father,
and *you shall be my sons and daughters,*
says the Lord Almighty." [See 2 Sam. 7:14.]

The rhetorical questions in 2 Corinthians 6:14–15 lay out five contrasts. The answer to each rhetorical question is a hard negative: there is no partnership between righteousness and lawlessness, there is no fellowship between darkness and light, Christ is not in agreement with Beliar, and believers and unbelievers do not share an understanding of God. Finally, as verse 16 says, there is no connection between the temple of God and idols. The reader is being encouraged to choose wisely.

Paul's statement "we are the temple of the living God" acts as a natural foil to the idols and idol worship that were present in the Corinthian culture of the day. At that time there were physical temples and temple rituals that were performed on behalf of local deities—the idols that Paul saw fit to warn against in the strongest (and cleverest) of terms. His mash up of the idea of temple and his addressees is a masterful conceptual blend, structured by the CONTAINMENT SCHEMA. The CONTAINMENT SCHEMA features a boundary, an enclosed area or volume, and an excluded area or volume. The in-and-out orientation is based on our bodily experiences in the world. It can also include the idea of objects that are located inside or outside of the container, as the enterprising baby in chapter 5 has demonstrated. In more abstract terms, containment features separation, differentiation, and enclosure.

Paul then goes on to elaborate by quoting God's own words to various audiences in the past, making them new for the Corinthians. New mental spaces are created at 6:16b with the phrase "as God said" and with the phrase "says the Lord" in 6:17. As previously mentioned, mental spaces can be structured by image schemas such as the CONTAINMENT SCHEMA discussed above. However, mental spaces can also be structured by **frame knowledge**, which is richer in detail. Frames are packets of knowledge that are readily available in our memory, such as an air travel frame, which would include arriving at the airport, dropping of the bags, going through security, getting on and off the plane, and leaving the airport. Mentioning one or two features of the frame will likely activate the whole frame. The statement, "I am going to the airport" will likely evoke the response, "I hope the security line isn't too long for you," or something similar.

Diagram 7.3 *Conceptual blending and the temple in 2 Corinthians 6:16*

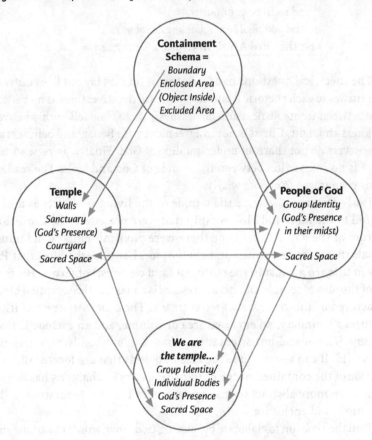

When Paul mentions "the temple of the living God," the phrase evokes a certain conceptual frame, that of worship. The sacral frame here includes an object of worship (the living God versus idols), and a sacred location (the temple). Other aspects of a sacral frame would be the worshippers and ritual. The sacral frame could be used to structure a worship situation in many different traditions—this frame could provide a basis for understanding a basic worship experience in the Jerusalem temple, up on the high hills, or in the individual temples to idols in Corinth. This raises a question of *identity* specific to this passage: What temple is Paul referring to when he confidently mentions the temple of God? If Paul were referring to the Jerusalem temple, what would that temple mean to the Corinthian believers? Since many of the Corinthian believers were gentile converts, they did not have the same cultural understandings and group memory of the Jerusalem temple that Paul carried as one who had trained with the rabbis in Jerusalem. For Paul, the Jerusalem temple would be a familiar model of sacred space—yet, in verse 16 he makes that abrupt turn—suddenly, the worshippers have become the location for worship.

Paul bolsters his line of thinking by a series of quotations and allusions to the Hebrew text that we know as the Old Testament and he does so by opening and connecting a series of mental spaces. He does this by quoting the words of God that had already been reported elsewhere. Our new mental spaces actually contain more mental spaces, as the quoted material had relevance in its first setting as well. Not all English translations clearly set out quotations, allusions, and echoes, but some study Bibles go into these issues and they are worth looking at more closely. It is entirely possible that Paul has compressed much more information into these verses than is obvious at first glance.

The initial mental space is created by the first direct quotation in 6:16, which reads **". . . as God said**, *'I will live in them and walk among them, and I will be their God, and they shall be my people.'"* This is a direct quotation of Leviticus 26:12, which is initially presented as God's words to Moses for his people, who were not yet in the promised land. Leviticus 26:1 starts with the instruction to refrain from making idols, so the entire chapter is on topic here. If the current addressees are the temple of God, they (the Corinthian believers) are to have nothing to do with idols either. The first echo is also included in 6:16, where the remark can be seen as a paraphrase of Ezekiel 37:27, which reads, "My dwelling place shall be with them; and I will be their God, and they shall be my people." The Ezekiel passage is presented as God's words to Ezekiel for the exiles. These statements speak clearly of God's desire to be present with his people. God's presence was especially evident in the tabernacle in the wilderness and, in later days, in the Jerusalem temple. With the exile, it became necessary to wrestle with the idea of physical location—where was the locus of God's presence for those in exile? The same question existed for the Corinthian believers, who saw temples for idols on nearly every corner—if not a physical temple, where might one encounter the living God?

A second mental space is opened with the direct quotation in 6:17, which states: "Therefore *come out from them, and be separate from them,* **says the Lord**, *and touch nothing unclean.*" This is a direct quotation of Isaiah 52:11, which is presented as God's words to the prophet for the exiles, who are being called to come out of Babylon—to separate themselves from any unclean thing as they go. Importantly, the choice to be separate is a big consideration here: given the choice between mingling with unclean things, the people are instructed to "not touch" and to willingly walk away. Finally, the phrase "and *you shall be my sons and daughters*" in verse 18 is an allusion to 2 Samuel 7:14, which is an iteration of God's covenant with David, spoken to David through the words of the prophet Nathan.

As this survey of the quotations and allusions in 2 Corinthians 6:16–18 notes, all the words are attributed to God and presented through the voice of one who speaks for God. Significantly the quotes and allusions are found in both the books of the Law (Leviticus) and the Prophets (Samuel, of the former prophets; Isaiah and Ezekiel, of the latter prophets). An interesting pattern develops because none of the original audiences had access to a physical temple. The Israelites coming out of Egypt had the mobile tabernacle. The exiles in Babylon had seen the destruction of the Jerusalem temple, and Paul himself was said to be a Pharisee, a sect that emphasized prayer and scripture over worship and ritual.

Ideas for Discussion

1. Read the story of Deborah and Barak in Judges 4:4–10. Look for space-building terms, such as verbs of speaking. Note aspects of the conversation between Deborah and Barak. Who is speaking in verse 6? Who is being quoted? Who is speaking in verse 8? In verse 9? How do each of these speech events open new mental spaces? What elements structure the spaces? How are the spaces connected? What is the overall effect of the conversation?

2. Read Psalm 23:1–4. Here the psalmist is comparing the Lord to a shepherd and himself to a sheep. What is the generic thought behind this comparison? In a sense, the comparison hinges on a caretaker and one being cared for. Is it possible to make this thought more generic yet? Think about creating a conceptual blending diagram that would contain these verses in the blended space. What elements would be contained in the source domain in input 1 (ideas about sheep herding)? What entities would be contained in the target domain in input 2? What connections can be made across these input spaces? What connections find their way into the blended space at the bottom, where the verses reside?

Further Reading

Two seminal volumes on Mental Spaces Theory are Gilles Fauconnier, *Mental Spaces: Aspects of Meaning Construction in Natural Language* (1994), and Gilles Fauconnier, *Mappings in Thought and Language* (1997). These volumes require a bit of heavy lifting but are worth looking into for the origins of the theory. For a look at how linguists incorporated Mental Spaces Theory into the analysis of various instances of language in use, see Gilles Fauconnier and Eve Sweetser, *Spaces, Worlds, and Grammar* (1996).

For the foundations of conceptual blending, see Gilles Fauconnier and Mark Turner, "Blending as a Central Process of Grammar" (1996). Gilles Fauconnier and Mark Turner's volume *The Way We Think: Conceptual Blending and the Mind's Hidden Complexities* (2002) is a delightful and accessible treatment of conceptual blending in the written word and in other real-life settings.

For embodiment and conceptual blending, see Mark Johnson, *The Body in the Mind: The Bodily Basis of Meaning, Imagination, and Reason* (1987), and Raymond W. Gibbs, *Embodiment and Cognitive Science* (2006).

Some of the earliest examples of conceptual blending and biblical studies are Bonnie Howe, *Because You Bear This Name: Conceptual Metaphor and the Moral Meaning of 1 Peter* (2006), and Elizabeth R. Hayes, "Of Branches, Pots and Figs: Jeremiah's Visions from a Cognitive Perspective" (2009). Howe's volume brings conceptual blending and cognitive metaphor theory to the table. Hayes's volume incorporates Mental Spaces Theory in her explanation of cognitive construction in the book of Jeremiah. A further example is Elizabeth R. Hayes, "The One Who Brings Justice: Conceptualizing the Role of 'the Servant' in Isaiah 42:1-4 and Matthew 12:15-21" (2012). Finally, a complete treatment of conceptual blending in 2 Corinthians 6:14-7:1 is found in Elizabeth R. Hayes, "The Influence of Ezekiel 37 on 2 Corinthians 6:14-7:1" (2007).

EIGHT

Connecting the Unrelated

The Ubiquity of Metaphor

This and That

Many of us have memories of sitting in a language or literature class, memorizing the difference between metaphor and simile. Many can still repeat "Simile is a comparison that uses 'like' or 'as,'" while metaphor is a comparison that does not use 'like' or 'as'" without stopping to think about it. Indeed, the presence or absence of "like" or "as" makes distinguishing between the two fairly easy. For example, Psalm 19:4b–5 contains a picturesque pair of similes that describe the rising of the sun and its path across the sky: "In the heavens he has set a tent for the sun, which comes out *like* a bridegroom from his wedding canopy, and *like* a strong man runs its course with joy" (NRSV). These lines capture the effect of a notable sunrise by comparing it to a proud groom exiting his tent after the wedding night, and to the sun's path across the sky as a daunting foot race run by a trained athlete, reveling in the experience. By way of contrast, Jesus's "I am" statements in John are metaphoric. For example, in John 15:1 Jesus states, "I am the vine." In this simple sentence Jesus is inviting his hearers to compare him with a growing plant. The comparison is more direct for metaphors, but the comparative function is the same: one entity is being understood in terms of another entity. The entity being explained is sometimes called the **target** and the entity used to explain is sometimes called the **source**.

Diagram 8.1 *Source and target domains*

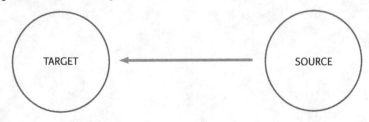

Our introduction to metaphor and simile may have taken place during a language or literature class and this might lead us to think that metaphor and simile are purely literary tropes. However, as it turns out, the analogical thinking that underlies these literary figures also underlies a great deal of the way we think and act in the world.

All about Conceptual Metaphor

Conceptual Metaphor Theory expands the literary understanding of metaphor by including comparisons between conceptual domains, which can be any coherent organization of experience. Thus, conceptual metaphors stand behind literary metaphors, but they can also be identified in other communications, such as advertisements, cartoons, and slogans. Analogical thinking is connected to our embodied experiences in the world. It is often schematic and structured by image schemas. For example, the conceptual metaphor LIFE IS A JOURNEY is structured by the SOURCE-PATH-GOAL SCHEMA: Life, like a journey, has a beginning, a trajectory, and an end. The correspondences, or conceptual mappings between birth with starting a journey, a life lived with the duration of the journey, and death with the completion of the journey are the essence of the metaphor. The name of the conceptual metaphor has propositional content, while the mappings themselves are a set of nonpropositional connections. In this way, the name of a conceptual metaphor such as LIFE IS A JOURNEY is a way to remember and recall the set of mappings itself. For this reason, conceptual metaphors note the correspondences between source domains and target domains. The domains contain rich knowledge that can be elaborated on in each situation.

Conceptual metaphors rely on information stored in long-term memory, such as image schemas, frames, and general encyclopedic background knowledge of the world. One aspect of this structured background knowledge is called the *Extended Great Chain of Being*, a hierarchy that goes back at least as far as Aristotle (see table 8.1 below). Kövecses notes that conceptual metaphor functions with the Extended Great Chain of Being metaphor system, which is based upon "a certain folk theory of how things are related to each other in the world" (Kövecses 2002, 126). He notes that this understanding likely goes back to the Bible. If this is the case, one likely biblical source for this ontological hierarchy is the story of creation in Genesis 1.

Table 8.1 *Extended great chain of being metaphor system*

God (Jewish-Christian tradition)	**(Creator)**
Cosmos/Universe	(Days 1–4)
Society	
ABSTRACT COMPLEX SYSTEMS ↑	
- -	- - - - - - - - - - - - - - -
Humans: *higher order attributes, behavior*	(Day 6)
Animals: *instinctual attributes, behavior*	(Day 6—land)
	(Day 5—sea/sky)
Plants: *biological attributes, behavior*	(Day 3)
Complex objects: *structural attributes—functional behavior*	
Natural physical things: *natural physical attributes and behavior*	

Significantly, the Extended Great Chain is not a metaphorical system in and of itself. Rather, it becomes a metaphorical system when one level of the chain is used to understand another level—one level becomes the source for understanding another level, the target. Such cognitive construal is evident in Genesis 1, where God exhibits attributes and behavior usually credited to humans in the Extended Great Chain—God speaks, God sees, and God evaluates. In this instance, human characteristics are used to understand the divine: humanity is the source for understanding the target, God. Another example of moving up the hierarchy is found in the taunt song regarding the idols of the nations found in Psalm 135:15-16, which reads: "The idols of the nations are silver and gold, the work of human hands. They have mouths, but they do not speak; they have eyes, but they do not see" (NRSV). Here the source domain of "complex objects" is used to understand the target domain, the idols. This is a pretty hefty insult! In these cases, the comparison moves upstream on the hierarchy. Importantly, the comparisons can move in either direction. The comparison runs down the hierarchy in Psalm 114:3-4, which reads: "The sea looked and fled; Jordan turned back. The mountains skipped like rams, the hills like lambs" (NRSV). In this instance, human and animal characteristics are the source used to understand the unusual behavior of the Red Sea, the Jordan River, the mountains, and the hills (the target).

Table 8.2 *Animacy hierarchy*

Speech act participant 1
Speech act participant 2
Speech act participant 3
Proper Noun
Animate
Inanimate
Mass

Linguists also use an animacy hierarchy in discussions of language proper and it can also be a useful tool for biblical studies.

Because conceptual metaphors account for correspondences between source domains and target domains, they may produce rather elaborate *extended metaphors* such as SOCIETY IS A PLANT. As mentioned above, the name of the conceptual metaphor has propositional content, while the mappings themselves are a set of nonpropositional connections. For the SOCIETY IS A PLANT metaphor, Kövecses notes that several mappings are possible (2002, 8):

Source: plant	Target: SOCIAL ORGANIZATION	Language in Use
(a) The whole plant	the entire organization	
(b) Part of the plant	part of the organization	*branch*
(c) Growth of the plant	growth of the organization	*is growing*
(d) Removing part	reducing the organization	*prune*
(e) Root of the plant	origin of the organization	*root*
(f) The flowering	the best stage	*blossom, flower*
(g) The fruit or crops	the beneficial consequences	*fruits*

Jeremiah 2:3 contains an instantiation of the SOCIETY IS A PLANT metaphor. It reads: "Israel was holy to the LORD, the *first fruits of his harvest.* All who ate of it were held guilty; disaster came upon them, says the LORD" (NRSV). The prophet notes that Israel was holy to the LORD. In a metaphoric elaboration, it is noted that Israel was the first fruits of the LORD's harvest. The first fruits were the first and best part of any harvest and were given to the priests as an offering. Israel was as special to God as the first part of the harvest that was devoted to him. Anyone who devoured Israel was considered to be guilty and was judged via disaster.

Conceptual metaphors such as the SOCIETY IS A PLANT metaphor play into abstract complex systems metaphors that speak to the way we think about social organizations, government, religious congregations, the workplace, and so forth. In addition to comparing these things to plants, it has been noted that the abstract complex system target domain can be understood through various source domains such as a MACHINE, a BUILDING, a PLANT, and a HUMAN BODY. The comparison in each of these is between a source that is lower on the hierarchy that is being used to understand a target that is higher on the hierarchy. The SOCIETY IS A PLANT complex system metaphor is particularly evident in biblical literature. From the prophetic indictment in Jeremiah 2:21–"Yet I planted you as a choice vine, from the purest stock. How then did you turn degenerate and become a wild vine?"– to Jesus's "I am" statement in John 15:1–"I am the true vine, and my Father is the vinegrower" (NRSV)–plant imagery abounds.

Complex system metaphors touch upon four major aspects of the system involved:

1. Does the system function effectively? [Jeremiah 2:21 would say no.]
2. Is it long lasting and stable?
3. Does it develop as it should? [John would say yes with proper encouragement.]
4. Is it in appropriate condition? [Kövecses 2002, 127]

Conceptual metaphor allows the author to address the condition of a society such as the Israelites, in an artistic and powerful way. The hyperbole created by referring to a society as a dying plant or a collapsed building is both attention getting and memorable.

The effect of hierarchical thinking on society and culture is worth considering: if hierarchy is ingrained in our background understanding of how the world functions, this is also likely reflected in the way we think about power and governance. This represents a challenge to the way we interpret ancient text in a modern world. Are there ways to reimagine these ingrained patterns and come up with some ideas about mutuality?

Short History

Conceptual Metaphor Theory is a large part of the cognitive turn that started in the last quarter of the twentieth century. George Lakoff and Mark Johnson's volume *Metaphors We Live By* (1980) introduced Conceptual Metaphor

Theory, and the volume represents the basis for what has followed in this area of study. Significantly, Conceptual Metaphor Theory has provided understanding of how analogical thinking gives rise to both literary and lived metaphors. Andrew Ortony's volume *Metaphor and Thought* (1993) provides an overview of Conceptual Metaphor Theory that situates the emergence of conceptual metaphor within the study of literary metaphor at that time. Zoltán Kövecses has distilled and elucidated Conceptual Metaphor Theory in his volume *Metaphor: A Practical Introduction* (2002) and followed that with a volume with Bálint Koller, *Language, Mind, and Culture: A Practical Introduction* (2006) that includes his thoughts about how society and culture both use and produce conceptual metaphor. These studies are readable and clearly presented.

Related Features in Biblical Studies

The areas of genre studies, imagery, and rhetorical studies all have points of contact with Conceptual Metaphor Theory. How we read the Bible is affected by the way we view the genre of the text. Whether we are reading the Bible as Scripture, as literature, or just as a plain good read, the genre of each part demands individual attention. C. S. Lewis famously noted that the Psalms are not theological treatises. The Old Testament/Hebrew Bible provides an interesting example. While the book of Daniel occurs in the Writings section of the Hebrew Bible, it occurs in the major prophets section of the Old Testament. The text is the same, but its position in the larger scheme of things is different. On the one hand, the reader of the Hebrew Bible may come to the text expecting story, whereas the reader of the Old Testament may expect prophecy. The conceptual blend between text and presupposition affects expectations.

Imagery in the Bible can be beautiful and uplifting:

> I saw the Lord sitting on a throne, high and lofty; and the hem of
> his robe filled the temple. (Isa. 6:1 NRSV)

It can be frightening and disturbing as well:

> Is Israel a slave? Is he a homeborn servant?
> Why then has he become plunder?

> The lions have roared against him,
> > they have roared loudly.
> They have made his land a waste;
> > his cities are in ruins, without inhabitant. (Jer. 2:14–15 NRSV)

What these images share is the use of metaphor, and the conceptual underpinning of these metaphors is both fascinating and worth further study.

Finally, rhetorical studies are concerned with the persuasive and emotional effects of the text and feature observation of the text from traditional rhetorical categories. Rhetorical studies are particularly useful for analyzing New Testament letters; however, entire studies have been done with Old Testament books as well. Again, metaphor can be used to gain attention and to strengthen certain points.

The Meaning of Conceptual Metaphor in Biblical Studies

Conceptual metaphor has much to contribute to biblical interpretation. There are three areas that stand out: metaphor and genre; metaphor and imagery; and metaphor and rhetoric. First, how we read the Bible depends on our presuppositions about the text. Is the text scripture? Is it literature? Does it have an overarching theme, or is it comprised of many themes? These are questions that have to do with genre and the Bible.

Discerning genre is often part of a close reading strategy, and indeed, the Bible itself acknowledges the difference between narratives, prophecy, writings, and poetry. Single literary metaphors are an expected part of reading the Bible and general metaphor theory suffices to explain some of the characteristics of single metaphors. Importantly, conceptual metaphor can extend the power of comparison to larger metaphor spaces, such as the "I am" statements in John. While the individual metaphors create interest, the entire complex creates understanding due to our ability to pull information from frame knowledge and other information stored in long-term memory. When conceptual metaphor structures a longer section of text, the imagery developed becomes richer as the text progresses. The story of Jesus as the gate in John 10:8–17 develops into an entire scenario that contains thieves and bandits, hired hands and sheep (see "Case Study: The Good Shepherd," below). Longer sections of text that are structured by conceptual metaphor also tend to use the metaphor space to develop details of a rhetorical argument. There is also much to be said for how individual literary metaphors draw upon conceptual metaphor as structured background knowledge. "The LORD is my shepherd" resonates across time and space, perhaps because the rich knowledge of the relationship between sheep and their caretakers is widespread and emotionally appealing.

Case Study: The Good Shepherd

Jesus's discourse in John 10:7–17 is structured by the PEOPLE ARE ANIMALS conceptual metaphor and by other animal husbandry imagery as well. It starts with Jesus's description of himself as the gate for the sheep in John 10:7. As a single metaphor, we can say that Jesus is the target and the gate for the sheep is the source. It is interesting that Jesus would describe himself in terms of a sheep gate, which in the ancient Near East was often an opening in the fence rather than a solid gate. However, the metaphorical statement also introduces a level of conceptual complexity for the larger passage. It is this conceptual complexity that Gavins describes as "double-vision" when she states:

> In order to understand the position that metaphors and their resultant blends take in the discourse as a whole, it is helpful to think about the processing of a blended world, whether it relates to micro-metaphor or an extended mega-metaphor, as a kind of conceptual double-vision. Whenever a metaphor occurs in a discourse our mental representation of the text in which the metaphor was generated continues and normally remains the prominent focus of our attention. This world, plus any further text-worlds created by the metaphor, feed into the blending process. (2007, 152)

While Gavins is working within a text-world perspective, we can back out a bit and discuss this text using metaphor theory with an added dash of conceptual blending (see chapter 7). The two spaces that are started with Jesus's statement can be viewed as a *reality space*, one that includes Jesus and his hearers. The second statement can be viewed as a metaphorical *speech space*—the world Jesus creates as he continues to use animal husbandry imagery as part of his discussion. We can then toggle between these spaces, or *worlds*, mentally blending as we read.

Table 8.3 *Double vision: the sheepfold metaphor in John 10:7–18*

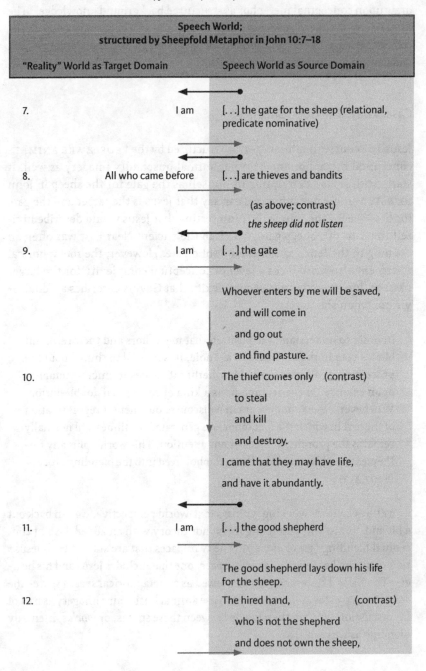

Speech World; structured by Sheepfold Metaphor in John 10:7–18	
"Reality" World as Target Domain	Speech World as Source Domain
7. I am	[. . .] the gate for the sheep (relational, predicate nominative)
8. All who came before	[. . .] are thieves and bandits
	(as above; contrast)
	the sheep did not listen
9. I am	[. . .] the gate
	Whoever enters by me will be saved,
	and will come in
	and go out
	and find pasture.
10.	The thief comes only (contrast)
	to steal
	and kill
	and destroy.
	I came that they may have life,
	and have it abundantly.
11. I am	[. . .] the good shepherd
	The good shepherd lays down his life for the sheep.
12.	The hired hand, (contrast)
	who is not the shepherd
	and does not own the sheep,

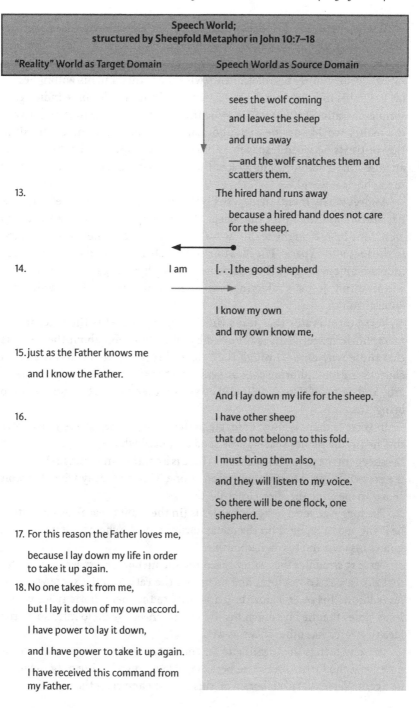

Speech World; structured by Sheepfold Metaphor in John 10:7–18	
"Reality" World as Target Domain	Speech World as Source Domain
	sees the wolf coming
	and leaves the sheep
	and runs away
	—and the wolf snatches them and scatters them.
13.	The hired hand runs away
	because a hired hand does not care for the sheep.
14. I am	[. . .] the good shepherd
	I know my own
	and my own know me,
15. just as the Father knows me	
and I know the Father.	
	And I lay down my life for the sheep.
16.	I have other sheep
	that do not belong to this fold.
	I must bring them also,
	and they will listen to my voice.
	So there will be one flock, one shepherd.
17. For this reason the Father loves me,	
because I lay down my life in order to take it up again.	
18. No one takes it from me,	
but I lay it down of my own accord.	
I have power to lay it down,	
and I have power to take it up again.	
I have received this command from my Father.	

Toggles between the reality space and the metaphoric space occur at verses 7, 8, 9, 11, 14, 15, and 17. The initial topic at verse 8 is Jesus himself. Likewise, the closing topic in verse 17 is Jesus himself. Verses 18–19 elaborate on Jesus, noting his relationship with the Father and his willingness to lay down his life. As a quick read down the reality world space indicates, a simple narration could say the same thing. However, the toggles between the reality world and the metaphorical world add color and emphasis to the contrasts between Jesus and "all who came before" and between Jesus and the "hired hand." Let us look at the color that is added by including the metaphorical world.

As previously mentioned, Jesus is the topic of verse 7, where he identifies himself as the gate for the sheep. This is followed by a contrast with "all who came before" in the reality space—they are called "thieves and bandits" in the metaphor space. The idea of a sheep gate in Jesus's day could simply indicate an opening in the enclosure, not a physical gate. If this is what was in mind, Jesus is referring to himself as an opening for the sheep to enter through.

Verse 9 reiterates that Jesus (in the reality space) is the gate (in the metaphoric space). This is followed by an elaboration about the benefits that those who enter through the gate will receive. This is followed by a contrast in metaphoric space at verse 10—the thief comes only to "steal, kill, and destroy." This is followed by yet another contrast—Jesus comes to bring life.

In verse 11 there is another toggle to the reality space, where Jesus states that he (in the reality space) is the good shepherd who lays down his life for the sheep (in the metaphoric space). There is a contrast in verses 12–13, where the erstwhile hired hand is described as one who runs away when the wolf shows up, leaving the sheep unprotected.

The toggle at verse 14 again has Jesus (in the reality space) declaring that he is the good shepherd (in the metaphorical space), where he states that he knows his own and his own know him.

Verse 15 straddles the reality space and the metaphoric space. Jesus notes that his Father knows him, and he knows the Father in the same way that Jesus knows his own, before toggling back to the metaphoric space where Jesus states that he lays down his life for the sheep. Verse 16 introduces the idea that Jesus has other sheep as well.

Verse 17 brings the toggling to an end in the reality space, where Jesus notes that the Father loves him because he lays down his life only to take it up again. Verses 18–19 elaborate on this thought and close the section.

Ideas for Discussion

1. Read Ephesians 4. Make some notes about what it means to live as the body of
   Christ. Would you consider this section to be an example of the SOCIETY IS A
   HUMAN BODY abstract complex system metaphor? If so, what characteristics
   of the four functional questions are addressed in this passage?

   a. What does it mean for this system to function effectively?
   b. Is it long lasting and stable?
   c. Is it developing as it should?
   d. Is it in the appropriate condition?

2. Read Ephesians 5:22-33. This passage has been considered troublesome due to
   some hierarchical thinking. Considering the way that the SOCIETY IS A HU-
   MAN BODY abstract complex system metaphor permeates this passage, can you
   re-envision the call for submission in words that would promote mutuality in
   relationships? Some possibilities may be "self-control," "mutual respect," and
   so on. Are these understandings supported by the text?

Further Reading

The cognitive turn that started in the last quarter of the twentieth century has
provided understanding of how analogical thinking gives rise to both literary
and lived metaphors. This turn is exemplified by the work of George Lakoff in
his volume *Women, Fire, and Dangerous Things: What Categories Reveal About
the Human Mind* (1987) and by his collaboration with Mark Johnson in *Metaphors We Live By* (1980) and *Philosophy in the Flesh: The Embodied Mind and
Its Challenge to Western Thought* (1999). These volumes represent the basis
for what has followed in the area of conceptual metaphor. Andrew Ortony's
volume *Metaphor and Thought* (1993) situates the emergence of conceptual
metaphor within the study of literary metaphor at that time.

   Zoltán Kövecses has distilled and elucidated conceptual metaphor in his
volume *Metaphor: A Practical Introduction* (2002) and followed that with a volume with Bálint Koller, *Language, Mind, and Culture: A Practical Introduction*
(2006). These studies are readable and clearly presented.

   Working with conceptual metaphor and longer stretches of text reflects
development from sentence level analysis to the analysis of longer stretches of
text. This movement was first seen in the area of discourse analysis and sub-

sequently found its way into analysis of metaphor as well. Robert E. Longacre explored the text at levels higher than a sentence in *The Grammar of Discourse* (1996) and *Joseph: A Story of Divine Providence: A Text Theoretical and Textlinguistic Analysis of Genesis 37 and 39-48* (2003). Margaret H. Freeman brought these insights to literary analysis in her essay "Cognitive Mapping in Literary Analysis" (2002), and Paul Werth's essay "Extended Metaphor—a Text-World Account" (1994) is an excellent connection between conceptual metaphor and full analysis of longer texts.

Conceptual metaphor has captured the imaginations of biblical scholars and the trickle of essays and presentations has grown into a flood. Individual essays and entire volumes have been written in the past few years, including Elizabeth R. Hayes, "Of Branches, Pots and Figs: Jeremiah's Visions from a Cognitive Perspective" (2009), and conference proceedings such as Antje Labahn, *Conceptual Metaphors in Poetic Texts: Proceedings of the Metaphor Research Group of the European Association of Biblical Studies in Lincoln 2009* (2013), and Pierre Van Hecke and Antje Labahn, *Metaphors in the Psalms* (2010). Conceptual metaphor is an excellent complement to biblical studies due both to the prevalence of literary metaphor in the Scriptures and to the nature of application of an ancient text to a modern age—embodiment is a key connection between the times and cultures of each setting.

NINE

Connecting the Related

The Power of Metonymy

What Do You Stand For?

Biblical stories, just as stories in general, feature protagonists and antagonists. In the book of 1 Samuel, these roles are played by the Israelites and the Philistines, respectively. The most famous battle scene is probably that between David and Goliath in chapter 17, but the two nations are in conflict also in chapter 4. The Israelites decide to bring the ark of the covenant to the camp to turn the outcome of the battle into their favor. Their reasoning is the following: if the ark is here, God will be here and then all will be well. And indeed, when the Philistines hear about the ark being in the camp of the Israelites, they are afraid for "God has come to the camp" (1 Sam. 4:7). Unexpectedly, however, the Philistines win the battle and take the ark with them, which results in some unpleasant events. After all, it is not just the ark they have moved but also God.

All about Metonymy

The story of the ark illustrates an important process for reading, that of mapping related categories unto each other. This prompts the Israelites to first speak of the ark and consequently replace this by God. Similarly, the Philistines connect the presence of the ark to the presence of God in the camp. Scholars call this transfer from one category unto another category within a single conceptual domain **conceptual metonymy**, or short, **metonymy**. Metonymy expresses a "stands-for relationship." The ark of the covenant in 1 Samuel 4–6 stands for God. The ark is the *vehicle entity* or **source**, God the *target entity* or **target**. In the particular case of the ark and God, one could categorize the relationship more generally as an example of LOCATION FOR

BEING. As we have seen for other intermediate categories, such as schemas and conceptual metaphors, also conceptual metonymies are written down with small capitals to indicate that they are knowledge structures rather than specific expressions in the text.

Diagram 9.1 *Metonymy as transfer within one domain*

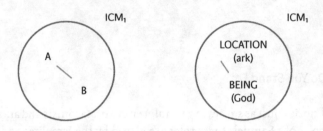

There are many *types of metonymies*. Some scholars group them more broadly into three categories, based on spatial, temporal, and causal relationships. Others produce extensive lists of up to forty-six different types of metonymy. The most common types are PART FOR WHOLE, WHOLE FOR PART, and CAUSE FOR EFFECT. But also PLACE FOR EVENT, OBJECT FOR USER, PRODUCER FOR PRODUCED, INSTITUTION FOR LOCATION, EVENT FOR PRECONDITION, PERSON FOR ROLE, and so on, are all examples of conceptual metonymies. Thus, when Elkanah asks his wife Hannah why she is sad at the opening of the book of 1 Samuel, he says "Why is your heart sad?" (1:8). Obviously, he wants to know why Hannah, as a person, is upset, rather than what is wrong with her heart. This is an example of a BODY PART FOR PERSON metonymy. Note that most English translations render the verse as "Why are *you* sad?," thus without the metonymy.

Diagram 9.2 *BODY PART FOR PERSON example*

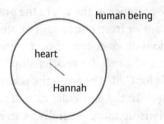

Metonymy is about *relationality*, which means that it is closely related to the other major conceptual feature that draws on relationships: **metaphor**. What is more, scholars nowadays think that metonymy may be more fundamental than metaphor. For example, when God is angry in the Hebrew Bible, the writers use the expression "his nose became warm." They rely on the conceptual metonymy EFFECT FOR CAUSE, here warm nose (body heat more generally) for anger. This evolves into the conceptual metaphor ANGER IS HEAT. This connection between metonymies and metaphors seems to be especially at work in cause-effect and whole-part relationships.

Whereas metonymy and metaphor are clearly related, they also have their differences. The most important difference is that metonymy happens within one conceptual domain, whereas metaphor connects two separate conceptual domains. To return to the sad Hannah in 1 Samuel 1, her heart and person are both part of the same conceptual domain of a human being. Hence, we are dealing with a metonymy. On the contrary, when Hannah thanks God in 1 Samuel 2 when dedicating her son, she says, "There is no rock like our God" (2:2). The rock and God form two different conceptual domains. They are connected because they share notions such as strength, solidity, eternity, and so on. The rock is not a part of God, nor is it a location representing God. In fact, it is Hannah who draws our attention to the possible connection between the rock and God.

Diagram 9.3 *Metonymy versus metaphor*

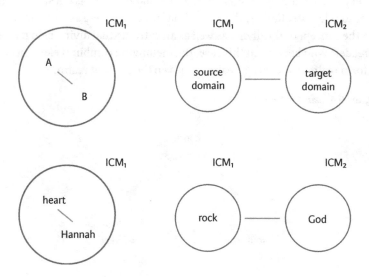

Another distinction is that metonymy is about *contiguity* while metaphor is dealing with similarity. Or more precisely, metonymy is about likeness of things that are already alike, such as a body part and a person. Metaphor, on the other hand, is generating similarity between things that are not by definition alike, such as a rock and a divine being. Scholars suggest a "is like/as if test" to distinguish between metaphor and metonymy, respectively. Thus, "Hannah's heart is like Hannah" does not make sense, but "Hannah's heart is as if it is Hannah" does. Similarly, "the rock is like God" works, contrary to "the rock is as if it is God."

A third difference has to do with the linguistic levels on which metonymy and metaphor work. Looking at the so-called **semiotic triangle** helps to understand this. The triangle visualizes the three elements that make up a linguistic sign: the word form (e.g., the word "heart" in a text), the concept (e.g., organ that rules the bloodstream), and the referent (e.g., a heart in the real world). Metonymy appears both within one of these realms and across realms. Metaphor only takes place between two concepts. As an example, consider Hannah's prayer in 1 Samuel 2. Hannah says, "My heart rejoices in the LORD" (2:1). Two metonymies are at work here. The BODY PART FOR PERSON is the one we have encountered before. Hannah's happiness is, like her grief, expressed by using a body part rather than her whole person. It goes without saying that Hannah herself is also praising the LORD, not just her heart. Both the heart and Hannah are part of the conceptual domain "human being," so the metonymy happens in the concept realm. In addition, there is a second metonymy with Hannah rejoicing in God. Whereas Hannah surely feels the character God's presence, the very fact of her praying suggests that the character God is not standing next to her to celebrate. Rather, the word "God" functions here as a metonymy for both the concept of the divine as well as an extra-textual divine being, at least for readers who believe. In this case, the metonymy combines elements from the form realm, the concept realm, and even the referent realm.

Diagram 9.4 *Semiotic triangle*

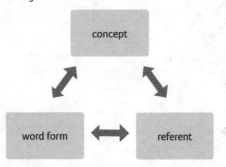

A last distinction entails the main function of both features. Scholars find that metonymy is more focused on directing attention while metaphor is primarily about understanding one thing through another. In other words, mentioning Hannah's heart rather than her whole person turns our attention to the emotional aspect of the phrase. It is not that we really need this reference to the heart to understand that when Hannah is sad, it is a matter of the heart rather than of the brain. In contrast, speaking of God in terms of a rock is precisely what facilitates the understanding of God. The comparison's prime objective is to help us comprehend God.

Finally, metonymy and metaphor often appear together in texts. They reinforce each other. In Hannah's prayer, metonymies such as the above (BODY PART FOR PERSON and WORD FOR CONCEPT) occur but also metaphors such as GOD IS A ROCK and GOD IS A PERSON (e.g., he casts and lifts up in 1 Sam. 2:8). Every single one of them gives information to the reader, helping to construe what the text means.

In the above, the contribution of metonymy to reading has already been touched on briefly. Metonymy guides readers' attention. Scholars have also noticed other functions, going from more literary ones to very pragmatic ones. Metonymies, for example, play an important role in **caricature**, in which body parts of a person are singled out and represent the whole being. More generally speaking, body parts can replace a person and become actors. Scholars speak of **metonymic agency** in that case. A good example is God's hand that replaces God frequently (discussed in the case study below). The hand acts on behalf of God, often combining this transfer of agency with an emphasis on God's power. Metonymies also fulfill pragmatic roles as far as discourse goes. They create *coherence* as well as *boundaries* in a text. The just mentioned example of the hand often occurs in a passage that starts off with mentioning God and using the phrase "the hand of God" before turning to "the hand." In other words, readers are given enough context to make sense of the metonymy and understand it as coherent within the text. What is more, the metonymy itself renders the text passage as well as God as a story character more comprehensible.

Short History

The ancient rhetoricians from Greece and Italy were probably the first ones to discuss metonymy. They treated it as a figure of speech. For a very long time, metonymy was understood in that way. Apart from extensive lists of examples from various sources, including the Bible, scholarship was limited to categorizing the examples. When cognitive linguists in the 1980s rediscovered metaphor, they also turned their attention to metonymy, but to a far lesser degree. In the basic works on metaphor by George Lakoff and Mark Johnson (1980) and later Zoltán Kövecses (2010), metonymy is discussed in a single chapter. The more recently published *Metonymy and Language* by Charles Denroche (2015) is one of the first book-length studies dedicated to metonymy, although with a good amount of metaphor study in it. This shows that the two phenomena are closely related and that discussing one cannot go without addressing the other. As linguists are shifting their attention from metaphor to other phenomena, such as metonymy, new insights will be gained over time.

Related Features in Biblical Studies

In biblical studies, metonymy mostly appears as a *rhetorical or literary figure*. As counts for the study of other stylistic figures, such as alliteration or parallelism, scholars have been eager to collect examples and categorize them. Such lists of metonymies exist for both Old Testament and New Testament texts. Certain metonymies have received a good amount of attention because of their ubiquity as well as theological or exegetical importance. One can think of the metonymy CITY FOR INHABITANTS, such as in Matthew 21:10 where "the whole city is stirred and asked." The inhabitants of the city are the true subject of the stirring and asking. Other common examples are various metonymies for God, for example HEAVEN FOR GOD as found in Mark 11:30 where the baptism of John is described as from heaven rather than from God.

Although metonymy is often treated as less literary than metaphor, the examples that have received attention in biblical scholarship tend to be precisely those that appear in poetic passages or have a more literary flavor to them. If these metonymies are of the types PART FOR WHOLE or WHOLE FOR PART, biblical scholars speak of synecdoche as a subtype of metonymy. The majority of biblical studies on the topic follows this distinction, even though outside biblical studies further research on the relationship between metonymy and synecdoche as well as which types of relationships they each represent has redefined the categories. Kevin Chau has incorporated these new insights in a 2014 piece on metonymy in Biblical Hebrew poetry. He shows exactly how understanding metonymy as a phenomenon can help readers in interpreting the biblical text. Even though he relies on cognitive-linguistic insights, his analysis acknowledges and foregrounds the poetic nature of the biblical passages he is studying. For example, Chau argues that Jeremiah 5:16 contains a conceptual metonymy rather than a flawed metaphor. The open tomb mentioned in the verse is a RESULT FOR SOURCE metonymy and the quiver a CONTAINER FOR CONTAINED metonymy. Together they serve to emphasize the deadliness of the invading Babylonians.

Finally, metonymy also plays a role in research that sees similarities between the form of the text and the form of the temple or the cosmos. Even though the term "metonymy" is lacking in these studies, these researchers are clearly describing a metonymic relationship between form and concept. This relationship combines different realms of the linguistic sign, or rather the larger text. The idea that the Hebrew Bible text replaces the physical temple when that temple is destroyed is probably the most obvious example. Again, this metonymy connects the realm of the form (the text as a whole here), the realm of the concept (the temple as safe haven, God's abode), and the realm of the referent (the actual temple in Jerusalem). Other examples are the metonymy of TABERNACLE FOR TEMPLE and CREATION NARRATIVE FOR PRIESTLY WORLDVIEW. In the case of the former, research has shown that the priestly account of the building of the tabernacle in Exodus 25–40 shows striking resemblance with ancient Near Eastern accounts of temple building in terms of its structure and setup. As far as the latter goes, the orderly creation found in Genesis 1 resembles the orderly worldview, both descriptive and prescriptive, found in the priestly regulations. Both examples establish a metonymic relationship beyond limited conceptual domains, such as a "person," but explore metonymy on a much broader level.

The Meaning of Metonymy in Biblical Studies

Metonymy is a subtle guide for the reader. Its process of making alike things more alike, so to say, requires less cognitive effort than the similarity play of metaphor. This means that metonymy may go unnoticed and its relevance underestimated. However, precisely as the other processes described in this book, most of which stay under the radar during a reading process, looking more closely at metonymy helps to understand how the biblical text produces meaning, or better, how readers come to a particular interpretation of the text.

There are a few areas and topics that would greatly benefit from a metonymic approach. First and foremost, metonymy (together with metaphor) appears all over when the Bible features the divine character God. God is compared to a plethora of things (rock, father, shepherd—all metaphors) and represented by stand-ins such as his hand, his height, his role as creator, and his word (all metonymies). A study of these examples and their occurrence will shed light on the biblical authors' idea about God. It shows how they deal with a special, divine, character in a narrative world that is human. The study of other biblical characters, especially but not solely, prophets, and the metonymies used for them can lead to new insights regarding their position. Which metonymies are used for which characters? For example, do prophets share certain metonymies with God? But also, do the metonymies for God change over time or depend on the biblical book chosen?

Another area that displays many metonymies is the realm of emotions. Emotional scenes often feature metonymy (and, again, metaphor). Questions to be asked here are: Are there patterns to be distinguished? For example, when do authors turn to metonymy and when to metaphor? And if patterns exist, do they run throughout the whole Bible or only parts of it? Is it only hearts that are happy or sad, or do we find other body parts, or even other metonymies, to express these specific emotions? And, as a constantly returning issue, do the metonymies make sense to modern-day readers or are they culture specific? We may feel happiness in our hearts, but do we also think in our hearts, as the biblical text goes (or would that rather be our mind or brain)?

The biblical text consists of different books and sources, pieced together over a significant period of time. Nevertheless, most readers consider the Bible (as Old Testament or New Testament or a combination of the two) as one book. In other words, they see it as a *coherent text*. Metonymy plays a crucial role in that perception. Expressions such as "after this" and demonstrative pronouns such as "that" are part of metonymic constructions of the type WORD FOR SCENE or WORD FOR EVENT. The scene or event mentioned is not just a single word but a whole chunk of text that has just been related or is about to be related. Tracking such connections more systematically explains the coherence of the biblical text. The above-mentioned metonymies for God play a cohesive role as well. Many of them appear at several places in the biblical corpus, bridging the gap between different books as well as between the Old Testament and the New Testament. For example, God's word, a metonymy for God, plays a crucial role in both Testaments.

Case Study: The Ark of the Covenant among the Philistines

In 1 Samuel 5, the Philistines take the ark of the covenant to the temple of Dagon, their god. As long as the ark is sitting in that temple, the statue of Dagon falls over several times. In addition, the community is affected by disease. The people decide to move the ark to a different place, Ekron. However, the people there are afraid the same will happen to them.

> ² And the Philistines took the ark of God and brought it into the temple of Dagon, and they set it next to Dagon. ³ And when the Ashdodites rose early the next day, see, Dagon was lying face down on the ground before the ark of the Lord. And they took Dagon and returned him to his place. . . .
>
> ⁶ And the hand of the Lord was heavy upon the Ashdodites, and he terrified and struck them with hemorrhoids, Ashdod and its territory. ⁷ When the people of Ashdod saw how matters stood, they said, "The ark of the God of Israel must not stay with us, for his hand is hard against us and our god Dagon."
>
> . . . ¹⁰ And they sent the ark of God to Ekron. . . .
>
> ¹¹ And they sent messengers too and gathered all the lords of the Philistines and said, "Send the ark of the God of Israel away, and let it return to its place, that it may not slay us and our people." For there was deadly panic in the whole city, so heavily had the hand of God been there. ¹² And the men who did not die were struck with hemorrhoids. And the cry for help of the city went up to heaven.

The story includes several examples of metonymy, beginning with that of the name of the god Dagon for its statue (NAME FOR STATUE). The first mention of Dagon in verse 2 refers to the god, but the second one to a cult statue of that god. Readers easily make that transfer because the god and his statue are part of the same conceptual domain of "deity." Similarly, readers understand that the Dagon lying face down in verse 3 is the statue, not the god himself. At the same time, the statue is not just a statue but represents the extra-textual deity (the *referent*). In that respect, the metonymy of Dagon crosses the realms of the linguistic sign. It is precisely because the statue is also the deity that the Philistines are so upset. This example not only gives us insight in ancient belief but also shows an awareness of the biblical authors of metonymy's, and in extension language's, power to affect not only the statue or the name of the god, but also the god himself.

Another metonymy appears in verse 7 with God's hand dealing with the people and Dagon. Obviously, it is not the hand but the being to whom the hand belongs that is affecting them. Here we have an example of the metonymy BODY PART FOR BEING. The expression "the hand of the Lord" in verse 6 assists readers in making the transfer. The metonymy creates textual coherence, because it picks up an expression that has been used before and adapts it. What is more, the hand is also metaphorically connected to power in the Bible. Therefore, singling out the hand of God, rather than another body part or God as a whole, directs the reader's attention to God's supremacy. Note that this metonymy of the hand draws on a personification of God. God is understood as a person with body parts like human beings. This example shows that metonymy and metaphor indeed can occur hand in hand. It also illustrates the idea of **metonymic agency**. In the Bible, God's hand very often represents and acts as stand-in for God.

In verse 10, a LOCATION FOR BEING metonymy is used when the ark is said to slay (or preferably not slay) the people of Ekron. In addition, a second metonymy appears when the city is mentioned rather than its inhabitants (PLACE FOR PEOPLE). Self-evidently, the people are panicking, not the material city. Similarly, in verse 12, the word "city" stands for inhabitants and even "heaven" could be said to stand for God here. Both metonymies are of the type LOCATION FOR BEING.

None of the discussed metonymies will come across to readers as particularly rhetorical or literary. This is partly because the text of 1 Samuel 5 is prose rather than poetry. The metonymies do not aim to embellish the text but are guides in reading. They focus readers' attention to deities and people through metonymic relationships with names, body parts, and locations. As far as the deities go, the metonymic expressions most certainly also aim to clarify these deities for the reader, at least as far as their contribution to the story goes. For example, the focus on God's hand draws attention to his power. Likewise, mentioning heaven focuses on the supreme position of God. One last thing to take away from this example is that the metonymies used for deities are similar to the ones for nondivine beings. The BODY PART FOR BEING metonymy is the same type we have seen for Hannah in 1 Samuel 1-2. And the LOCATION FOR BEING metonymy at the end of the chapter appears for both the inhabitants of the city and God.

Ideas for Discussion

1. Metonymies often go unnoticed unless you start looking for them actively. Find examples in the following verses. Can you discern the specific type of metonymy for each of the examples? What can you say about possible functions of each metonymy?

1 Samuel 2:27: And a man of God came to Eli and said to him, "Thus said the LORD: 'Did I truly reveal myself to your father's house when they were in Egypt subject to the house of Pharaoh?'"

Mark 14:61: Again, the high priest asked him: "Are you Christ, the son of the Blessed One?"

Matthew 27:4: I have sinned, for I have betrayed innocent blood.

2. Metonymies first appeared as rhetorical figures in ancient rhetorical treatises. In other words, these people considered metonymy to be persuasive, emphatic, or embellishing in nature. Consider the following passage from the Sermon on the Mount in Matthew 5:38-42. Can you identify the metonymies? Would you characterize any of them as rhetorical? Why or why not?

[38] You have heard that it was said, "An eye for an eye and a tooth for a tooth." [39] But I say to you, "Do not resist the one who is evil." But if anyone slaps you on the right cheek, turn to him also the other. [40] And if anyone wants to sue you and take your tunic, let him have your cloak as well. [41] And if anyone forces you to go one mile, go with him two miles. [42] Give to the one who begs from you, and do not refuse the one who would borrow from you.

Further Reading

A general introduction to metonymy can be found in Zoltán Kövecses's book *Metaphor: A Practical Introduction* (2010, 171-94), and George Lakoff and Mark Johnson, *Metaphors We Live By* (2003, 35-40). Categorizations of the different types have been suggested by various pieces in the book *Metonymy in Language and Thought*, edited by Klaus-Uwe Panther and Günter Radden (1999). In order of appearance these are Günter Radden and Zoltán Kövecses, "Towards a Theory of Metonymy"; Andreas Blank, "Co-presence and Succession: A Cognitive Typology of Metonymy"; and Brigitte Nerlich, D. Clarke, and Z. Todd, "'Mummy, I Like Being a Sandwich': Metonymy in Language Acquisition." Another categorization can be found in Abdul Al-Sharafi, *Textual Metonymy: A Semiotic Approach* (2004).

More recent studies of metonymy focus on its functionality. Paul Simpson discusses stylistic functions, in particular metonymic agency, in *Stylistics: A Resource Book for Students* ([2004] 2014, 44-46). Discourse coherence is addressed in Zhengling Fu, "The Application of Conceptual Metonymy in Discourse Coherence" (2016), and Antonio Barcelona, "The Role of Metonymy in Meaning Construction at a Discourse Level" (2007). Anna Truszczyńska addresses metonymy and boundaries in *Conceptual Metonymy: The Problem of Boundaries in the Light of ICMs* (2002). Charles Denroche addresses several functions in his *Metonymy and Language: A New Theory of Linguistic Processing* (2015), as does Raymond W. Gibbs in "Experiential Tests of Figurative Meaning Construction" (2007).

Denroche offers an overview of previous linguistic research on metonymy (2015, 56-80). For metonymy and classical rhetoric, see Luigi Arata, "The Definition of Metonymy in Ancient Greece" (2005).

For metonymy and biblical studies, one can turn to the following pieces: S. Vernon McCasland, "Some New Testament Metonyms for God" (1949), and Carl D. Dubois, "Metonymy and Synecdoche in the New Testament: A Revision and Augmentation of John Beekman's 'Metonymy and Synecdoche'" (1999). Kevin Chau combines literary and cognitive insights in his piece "Metaphor's Forgotten Brother: A Survey of Metonymy in Biblical Hebrew Poetry" (2014). Examples of metatextual metonymies can be found, among others in, Victor A. Hurowitz, "The Priestly Account of Building the Temple" (1985), and Mark S. Smith, *The Priestly Vision of Genesis 1* (2010, 108-14).

PART THREE

The Process of Reading a Text

TEN

Reading in Context

The Role of Discourse Worlds

Who's Reading?

It is a sunny Sunday afternoon, an excellent time to read a piece of lovely love poetry from the Bible. I sit on the deck, the kid playing in the background. There is a light breeze, a smell of summer in the air. I hope the kid will leave me this little moment to read a bit of the Song of Songs. It may not have been written on a sunny day on the weekend, but some of its scenes feel as if they could fit right into my backyard, or at least, in the field behind it.

All about Discourse Worlds

Texts are always read in a specific, real-life context. This is no different for the Bible. When you pick up the book, it is a particular day and a specific moment in your life. You are at a certain place; with all the things you know and feel at that point in time. This immediate situational context surrounding the reading of the Bible is what scholars refer to when they speak of the **discourse world**.

Diagram 10.1 *Discourse world of a written text*

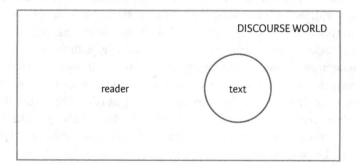

The discourse world is the world in which a specific reader engages with a text. It consists of at least two participants and their perceptions. So, when I am describing myself sitting on the deck reading the Song of Songs, I am describing the discourse world of my reading. This world has a specific setting: a sunny Sunday afternoon, a backyard, and a deck. I am a participant in the reading event, experiencing the breeze, the sun, and the smell of summer. I also see my kid playing in the backyard.

In the case of reading a text, the second participant is the author. Since this author is, by definition, absent, readers create a substitute for this author. This substitute could be the narrator of the text or a character, depending on how the story is told. In any case, readers communicate with a text in ways similar to a face-to-face conversation. For face-to-face conversations, the discourse world includes both participants. However, for written texts, the world of the author (substituted by the narrator or a character) is different from that of the reader. One speaks in that case of a **split discourse world**.

Diagram 10.2 *Split discourse world of a text*

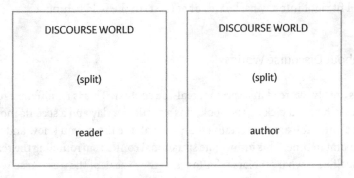

Scholars have distinguished the following elements to be part of the discourse world: *knowledge, beliefs, hopes, dreams, memories, imaginations, intention,* and *perceptions* (see diagram 10.3 below). Most research has paid attention to the knowledge item. Readers bring certain knowledge to the text. They do not come empty-handed. Regarding the biblical text, this knowledge has often been an issue of debate. Can readers understand the Song of Songs properly, just relying on their sunny Sunday afternoon setting, as I described mine above? Or do they need other knowledge in order to understand the Song? What is the role of historical knowledge or literary knowledge (the genre of love poetry), for example? Do you need to have experienced love to read the Song?

Diagram 10.3 *Elements of the discourse world*

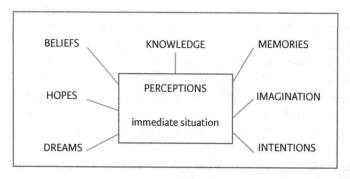

Knowledge comes in different forms. *General knowledge* includes *linguistic and cultural knowledge*. For the Song, this means you understand the language of the poem, the meaning of its style as well as the cultural prototypes it belongs to. In biblical scholarship, this kind of knowledge is often called background knowledge. It is what you are taught when you take a class on, say, the Song of Songs. Yet, general knowledge also includes your own knowledge about how language works, not just in the Song, but in communication in general, and your (cultural) knowledge about love, poetry, cities, and the countryside, for example. In addition, there is *perceptual and experiential knowledge*. Things you know because you have perceived and experienced them. The Song's sensory world certainly evokes knowledge of that kind and invites readers to dig into their own previous sensations. Since readers are communicating with the text, they may also gain new knowledge from the text. As such, knowledge moves from the private sphere of one participant to the public, shared sphere of two or more participants. This process is called **incrementation**.

Diagram 10.4 *Knowledge and Song of Songs*

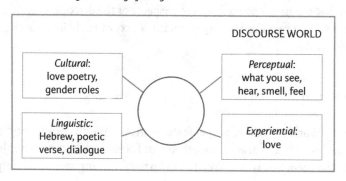

The knowledge of readers seems like an extremely broad source of information. How will we be able to determine which knowledge a reader applies when reading the Bible, and thus which knowledge affects the understanding of the text? Will this knowledge not be highly dependent upon the individual reader? The answer is it will not. Yes, readers have a vast knowledge store, which is individually determined to a certain degree, but texts narrow that storage down considerably. When you read a text, only the relevant areas of knowledge for that particular text are activated. This is the *principle of text drivenness* at work. For example, when I read the Song of Songs, I do not need knowledge about cooking dinner or playing the piano. Yet, my knowledge about love, cities, and the outdoors will come in handy. Likewise, another reader may know a lot about computers or science fiction movies, but, again, what the text will activate is knowledge that has to do with love, cities, and the outdoors.

As diagrams 10.3 and 10.4 above show, readers bring more than just knowledge to the table. These other elements, such as beliefs or dreams or memories, have been the object of study more recently. Several of them have been identified as emotive in nature. They have to do with readers' *emotional response* to texts. This response is the result of an interaction between the reader and the text. When you read the opening lines of the Song of Songs in its original Hebrew version, one *sh*-sound follows another. This sound repetition immediately draws a reader's attention, away from their world into the world of the text. What is more, the specific sound chosen has a comforting as well as an enticing effect. It is okay to turn to the world of the Song, forget about your world for a moment. When the text consequently describes the kisses of a lover's mouth, the reader is already in the right state of mind. The sound as well as the content will have evoked memories of youth loves or that first kiss. These memories will engage the reader even more. They will intensify the effect of the poem. This example clearly shows that the non-knowledge-based aspects of the discourse world play as much a role in reading and experiencing a text as traditional background knowledge does.

Short History

Discourse worlds appear as proper features in Paul Werth's work (1995, 1999). Discourse worlds do not generate a theory or framework in themselves but are part of the theory of which Werth will be the founding father, namely Text

World Theory (see chapter 12). Whereas most scholarship on texts pays some attention to the reader's world, mostly referred to as the extra-textual world or a similar term, literary studies tend to leave it with that. The meaning of the text is something that exists regardless of the reader. Werth shows that such is not the case. What is more, he argues that reading always requires a discourse world that necessarily interacts with the world of the text. Werth, and for that matter, many after him, focus on the element of knowledge in the discourse world. It is only more recently, with studies focusing on the emotive response of readers to texts (e.g., Stockwell 2009), that elements such as beliefs and hopes of readers have come into the scholarly picture again.

Related Features in Biblical Studies

The extra-textual world has always been a major concern in biblical studies. It has been referred to as context and *Sitz im Leben*. Traditional scholarship points with these terms to the original setting of the text and the original audience, in other words, the initial discourse world. This kind of scholarship aims to reconstruct that setting in order to understand the text better. Underlying this presumption is the idea that the meaning of the text is influenced by the context in which it is produced and read. For example, the two creation narratives that open the book of Genesis stem from two different contexts. In one context, that of the first narrative, order and rules are important. They served to get a grip on life in less controllable times. This setting required a God character who was in charge, one who kept the oversight and made sure everything would be okay in the end. The circumstances in which the second creation narrative was written were different; there were no big threats. As a result, we see a story that focuses more on the one-on-one relationship between God and human beings. The two creation narratives show that the different discourse worlds of the writers lead to the production of different stories. It goes without saying that such also counts in the case of readers: different discourse worlds result in different interpretations.

Scholars studying the *reception history* of the text have made the latter their primary object of research. They analyze how certain stories are received over time in various art forms. And they reflect on how the specific time, place, makers, and intended audiences of these pieces of art have influenced the interpretation of the stories as found in the pieces. Again, what these studies analyze is the role of the discourse world in the understanding of a biblical story. Depending on the time and place, the figure of Mary Magdalene, for example, has been identified as a prostitute and a sinner, but also as a powerful woman.

A third group of researchers with an interest in the discourse world are those who ask about the meaning and relevance of the Bible for current-day readers. Often their interpretations draw on a contrast between the ancient discourse world and the contemporary world. For example, the changed perspectives on violence render a lot of biblical stories problematic for current-day readers. Can someone like Jael be a heroine when she achieves her goal through murder? What is at stake here is exactly the split discourse world mentioned before, the fact that the discourse world of the author(s) is significantly different from that of the modern reader. One way to resolve this tension is to provide a **counterreading**. Such a reading consciously goes against the unconscious process of integrating the discourse world of writer and reader. It wants to prevent readers from adopting the ideas of the text. Note that this not only happens with biblical texts, but also with works by authors who, for example, write negatively about women or immigrants. Thus, a counterreading for Jael's story in Judges 4–5 would be one that openly condemns the violence committed by Jael. As a result, readers will not identify so easily with this character and, hopefully, not commit similar violence themselves.

The Meaning of Discourse Worlds in Biblical Studies

As the above overview shows, discourse worlds have always been part of biblical studies. Scholars have been and are aware that context is key to interpretation. In the quest for the meaning of the Bible, they have often privileged the original setting over other settings. In doing so, they have overlooked the fact that all readings are contextualized, including scholarly ones interested in the ancient readership. Discourse worlds can help us evaluate different interpretations of the text critically. They form a tool to assess the interpretation history of the Bible. For example, why do scholars initially pay little to no attention to the sexual connotations in the story of Jael and Sisera's encounter? When does this change, and what prompts this shift? And how is the story received in current-day scholarship, in the age of #MeToo?

This last question is a leg up to another area where discourse worlds, and especially the notion of the split discourse world, can help: reading the Bible in the contemporary world. Rather than reading uninformed, we can reconstruct the authors' discourse world for a particular Bible passage as well as ours. Obviously, as soon as we enter the more emotional parts of the schema presented in diagram 10.3, it will involve some guesswork, but nevertheless, contemporary readers will be able to reconstruct some of it. For example, the text under study is the letter of Paul to the Philippians. Paul writes this letter in isolation. He reaches out in a time of duress. When a reader nowadays finds themselves in precarious circumstances, some elements of the discourse world of Paul will overlap with that of the reader. As a result, the split discourse world will be less split, and readers will feel more connected to the world of the text. Following the same process, when readers have not experienced any kind of isolation, they may have a harder time bridging the gap between the discourse world of Paul and that of themselves.

Obviously, bridging the gap does not mean accepting whatever the text says. Modern-day readers do live in a different world, where, for sure, some things have changed for the good. Yet, as readers, we are invited to set those changes next to the discourse world of the biblical text. We are invited to bring both discourse worlds to our reading of the text. The notion of discourse worlds does not change our world, nor does it affect our initial emotional responses to the text. However, they do allow us to try and understand why we feel the way we feel about the text. And why other people may respond differently to the same text. And why an ancient audience may have responded differently.

Discourse worlds are perhaps the trickiest part of reading the Bible. They consist of various elements, some of which we may not be aware. They include the famously known historical background knowledge, but also the overlooked real reader with their ideas, beliefs, dreams, and feelings. What is more, every reading of the biblical text draws on these discourse worlds. They actively, although perhaps silently, contribute to what readers come up with as meaning of a particular biblical passage. Therefore, they deserve our attention.

Case Study: The Song of Songs

One of the more famous passages of the Song of Songs is the description of a female body in chapter 4. Similar descriptions appear in other chapters of the Song. The speaker is addressing another character, a woman, as the body parts and gendered language (at least in Hebrew) reveal. These are elements of the text world, the world created by the text, as we will see in chapter 12.

The interpretation of this text world is influenced by the discourse world of the reader.

> [1] Behold, you are beautiful, my love,
>   behold, you are beautiful.
> Your eyes are doves behind your veil.
> Your hair is like a flock of goats
>   that leap down Mount Gilead.
> [2] Your teeth are like a flock of ewes
>   that go up from the washing.
> All of them bear twins
>   and none of them has lost its young.
> [3] As a crimson thread are your lips
>   and your mouth is lovely.
> As a pomegranate split open
>   is your brow behind your veil.
> [4] As the tower of David is your neck
>   built to hold weapons,
> a thousand shields hang from it
>   all the round shields of the warriors. (Song 4:1-4)[1]

As argued above, the biblical text has a split discourse world: the world of the author(s) and that of the reader. The author's world is reconstructed based on information scholarship has collected. Thus, we know that the *cultural* context of the Song is one of love poetry. There are similar poems in other ancient Near Eastern traditions, for example in Sumerian. There may also be a connection with an invective genre that presents itself as flattery, as found in the Arabic tradition. Both elements shine through in the passage above. The text speaks of beauty and darlings and describes the female body in detail as only lovers would do. At the same time, the comparisons may be hiding a critique. Should a king not be focusing on war and battle, as verse 4 suggests, rather than thinking of love and women? *Linguistic* knowledge involves the choice of words typical of love poetry as well as the use of typical poetic devices such as **parallelism**, as found at the end of verse 1 and the beginning of verse 2, or a **chiasm**, a reversed parallelism, as between the opening of verses 2 and 3. In addition, this passage is presented as discourse directed to a particular person, who will later respond to the speaker in a similar manner. Indications of *perceptual* knowledge are the

---

1. All translations in this chapter are the author's own.

image of a flock of goats coming down a mountain or the intensity of the red color of her lips. *Experiential* knowledge may entail both being in love as well as tending a flock or even visiting the citadel of David.

Let us now turn to the discourse world of the reader, being me. As a Bible scholar, I am aware of most of the linguistic and cultural knowledge that makes up the discourse world of the Song. I also know that, in addition to a love poem or an invective, some have read the poem allegorically. This means that they consider the two lovers to stand for something else, namely God and his church. However, imagine I did not know about all of this. What would I bring then to the text? In other words, which knowledge would be activated? I would say, love and dialogue would be two elements. Clearly, the language indicates that there is a lover speaking. The comparisons may sound a little weird. They may not match my definition of love poetry. Nevertheless, I can still see where they are coming from, because I have seen flocks grazing on a mountainside and in my very short ballet career as a seven-year-old some people used to say I had a very nice long neck. So, I understand that many shields on a neck represent that long neck some people consider a trait of beauty. Both these examples no longer draw on the general knowledge we discussed before, but on perceptual and experiential knowledge. I use what I have experienced and perceived before to understand what the text wants to tell me.

When I read the text, all the above will influence how I eventually interpret the text. What is more, emotional elements from the discourse world, such as memories or beliefs, will play a role as well. Did that comment about my long neck make me feel good? If so that may color my reading of verse 4 positively. On the contrary, if it made me feel uncomfortable or unhappy, I may interpret verse 4 in a more negative light, perhaps even as an insult. These are just a few examples to show how discourse worlds make their way into reading the Bible. As a final note, discourse worlds show how complex reading as a process is, and how many elements contribute to what we consider to be the meaning of a text.

Ideas for Discussion

1. Consider the role of discourse worlds in the opening of Nahum 3 (vv. 1-6). What is the context of this passage? Which knowledge did the writer rely on when he wrote this prophecy? Think about historical background (about the city's fall), but also about cultural knowledge (the connection with the book of Jonah, the personification of the city), as well as perceptual and experiential

knowledge (witnessing a fight, for example). How much of this knowledge did you have as a reader? Did the lack of certain knowledge influence your understanding of the text?

2. Read the story of Judith in the Apocrypha book of Judith (Jth. 8–16). Write down your initial response. What is the text about and how did it make you feel? Read the story a second time and make notes next to the text as you progress. Can you indicate which discourse world elements are activated by the text? Which kind of knowledge do you use? Does the text evoke certain memories or dreams (or other elements from diagram 10.3)? How do any of these elements influence your response to the text? Compare with your classmates.

3. Not only scholars but also various artists have voiced their opinion about Judith. Compare the following pieces: Judith relief of the cathedral of Chartres (thirteenth century); "Return to Betulia" by Boticelli (1472); "Judith" by Klimt (1901 and 1909); "Judith kills Holofernes" by Artemisia Gentileschi (1620); "I'll make you shorter by a head" by Tina Blondell (1999); and Wiley's Judith (2012). Look up the background of the artists. Can you indicate how the discourse world of the artist has shaped the final portrayal of Judith in their work? How does this portrayal match or deviate from what you have come up with in your text study?

Further Reading

Discourse worlds are an integral part of Text World Theory. The two basic works to turn to are Paul Werth, *Text Worlds: Representing Conceptual Space in Discourse* (1999), and Joanna Gavins, *Text World Theory: An Introduction* (2007). They both have a good discussion of discourse worlds with examples. Werth introduced the various elements of the discourse world first in "How to Build a World (in a Lot Less Than Six Days and Using Only What's in Your Head)" (1995, 52). More recent works that focus on some of the aspects other than participant knowledge are Ernestine Lahey, "Text-World Landscapes and English-Canadian National Identity in the Poetry of Al Purdy, Alden Nowlan, and Milton Acorn" (2005); Peter Stockwell, *Texture: A Cognitive Aesthetics of Reading* (2009); and Sara Whiteley, "Text World Theory, Real Readers and Emotional Responses to *The Remains of the Day*" (2011).

The background of the Bible is discussed in the following introductory volumes: Michael Coogan, *A Brief Introduction to the Old Testament: The Hebrew Bible in Its Context* (2009); John Barton, ed., *The Hebrew Bible: A Critical Companion* (2016); Mark A. Powell, *Introducing the New Testament: A Historical,*

Literary, and Theological Survey (2018); and John Barton, *The Bible: The Basics* (2019). The term *Sitz im Leben* goes back to Hermann Gunkel and his study of the original setting of the Psalms in *The Psalms: A Form-Critical Introduction* ([1926] 1967). A general introduction to the reception history of the Bible is *The Oxford Handbook of the Reception History of the Bible* (Lieb, Mason, and Roberts 2011). Nice examples of more focused works are Colleen Conway's *Sex and Slaughter in the Tent of Jael: A Cultural History of a Biblical Story* (2017) and Cheryl Exum's *Art as Biblical Commentary: Visual Criticism from Hagar the Wife of Abraham to Mary the Mother of Jesus* (2019). Examples of counter-readings are Athalya Brenner and Carole Fontaine, *A Feminist Companion to Reading the Bible: Approaches, Methods and Strategies* (1997), and Fernando F. Segovia and R. Sugirtharajah, *A Postcolonial Commentary on the New Testament Writings* (2009).

A short selection of various interpretations of the Song of Songs are Francis Landy, *Paradoxes of Paradise: Identity and Difference in the Song of Songs* (1983); Elie Assis, *Flashes of Fire: A Literary Analysis of the Song of Songs* (2009); Scott B. Noegel and Gary Rendsburg, *Solomon's Vineyard: Literary and Linguistic Studies in the Song of Songs* (2009); Christopher Meredith, *Journeys in the Songscape: Space and the Song of Songs* (2013); and Elaine T. James, *Landscapes of the Song of Songs: Poetry and Place* (2017).

ELEVEN

Reading as Imagining Different Worlds

The Meaning of Possible Worlds

What If Oranges Were Blue?

The book of Ezekiel is well-known for its elaborate and fantastic visions. These evoke worlds inhabited by creatures no one has ever encountered in real life and with features no real world has. In the opening vision, for example, Ezekiel is describing winged creatures with four heads. Are they real or not? What are they? As readers we can surely imagine such beings. We can even draw them. Although they may be surreal according to the biological rules of our own world, they are possible in our mind.

All about Possible Worlds

Ezekiel's visions form an excellent example of what scholars have called possible worlds. A **possible world** is an alternative to the actual or real world. Or otherwise put, our **actual world** (AW) is only one of a number of possible worlds. Each world functions by its own rules and premises. Thus, the winged creatures in the opening vision of Ezekiel may be impossible in our real world, because creatures cannot be human and animal at the same time, nor can they have four heads, and so on. However, there might be a world in which such creatures can exist.

For texts, the **textual actual world** (TAW) forms the center of a story. Readers generally assume that this textual actual world is similar to the actual world they are living in, unless otherwise indicated in the text. Thus, before Ezekiel has his first vision, the world of the text is not so different from the world of the reader. The time indication is familiar (fifth day of the fourth month), there is a location (near the Chebar Canal), and so on. In addition to this actual world, writers (including Ezekiel) can evoke alternate possible worlds (APWs). Ezekiel's first vision is such a world. It is a world in which strange creatures live and Ezekiel is informed about future events.

Diagram 11.1 *Actual world and alternative possible worlds*

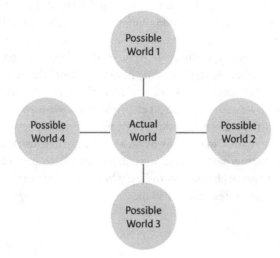

Diagram 11.2 *Actual and possible worlds in Ezekiel*

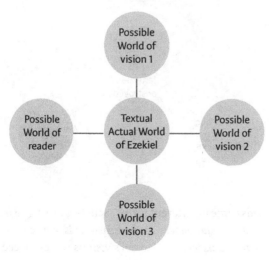

Statements about worlds are always evaluated within their world. Something is true or false in a certain world, but not necessarily in another one. If statements turn out to be false, readers deal with an **impossible world**. Note that this means that the world violates its own rules. In other words, the term refers to the logical construction of a world, not to its imaginative setup. Ezekiel creates a fantastic world in his visions, but as long as it is internally coherent, this world remains possible. The best example is the final vision of the rebuilt Jerusalem. Since the Jerusalem of the actual world is destroyed at that point in time, one could say that the vision is at odds with this reality. However, the Jerusalem imagined by the vision is coherent. At no point does it violate the rules within the world of that apocalyptic future Jerusalem. Therefore, it is a possible world. That is precisely what readers over time have taken from this text: its message of possibility rather than its apparent conflict with a particular actual world.

The vision of Jerusalem is also an example of a **counterpart**. When several versions of the real world at different points in time are evoked by a text, they form counterparts. In the book of Ezekiel, the possible world of Jerusalem at the end is a counterpart of the Jerusalem described in other chapters, most notably, the images in chapters 16 and 23, where Jerusalem's wicked behavior is presented as probable cause of its fall.

Diagram 11.3 *Counterparts*

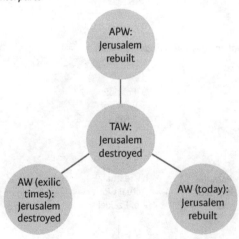

Possible worlds come in different forms. Scholars distinguish the following types: *desire worlds, obligation worlds, fantasy worlds, epistemic worlds (knowledge)*, and *goals and plans worlds*. Ezekiel's visions can be placed in several of these categories, depending on the position taken. For example, the first vision may come across to some readers as a fantasy world with nonexisting creatures. Others may interpret the world as a goals and plans world of God. From Ezekiel's point of view, it could be an obligation world, because it represents his duty. Regardless of the precise label, all these categorizations indicate a hypothetical world different from the textual actual world in which Ezekiel is having the vision. As we will see later (see "Case Study" below), the text offers cues to determine which possible world readers are dealing with. At the same time, one should not forget that readers play a role in the interpretation of the text, and thus also of its possible worlds, as repeatedly shown in the previous chapters.

Possible worlds are inherent to storytelling. As the list above shows, not all of them are as obvious as the visionary worlds in Ezekiel. However, for these alternate worlds to work for readers, it is important that these worlds are *close* to the reader. Closeness should be understood in terms of *accessibility*. Can readers access the time, objects, physical laws, and language found in the alternate world? As we have seen elsewhere, the **principle of minimal departure** comes into play again. Readers take their own world as the starting point. Any step outside of it requires an effort. If that effort is too big, for example, when the described world has unknown objects, time, physical laws, and language, readers will not be able to construe the world, regardless of it being possible or impossible. To return to the book of Ezekiel, readers will consider the final vision of Jerusalem accessible, even though it is a possible rather than an actual world that is described. The features of the city are similar to features of other ancient cities. The way the city is built is not new. The language used to describe the urban space is language readers know from other building accounts and passages in the biblical corpus, such as the building of the temple of Solomon or the construction of the tabernacle. All these elements make the possible world of the vision accessible to readers.

What is new in this future Jerusalem is the peace and the lack of sin. It takes a **re-centering** of the reader to incorporate that new information. This brings us from what possible worlds are to what they mean for the reading process. When readers re-center, they leave the (textual) actual world and adopt the possible world proposed in the text as their new (textual) actual world. In the case of Jerusalem, this means that readers adopt the city imagined by Ezekiel as a replacement for whatever Jerusalemite world they had set as their initial actual world. This process of re-centering leads to **immersion** into the text: a reader merges their actual world with the possible world of the text, and, as a result, experiences a feeling of being integrated into the textual world. According to literary theorists, the key to this process lies in the reader's acceptance of the created world to be possibly real.

Short History

The idea of possible worlds goes back to the theological philosophy of Gottfried Leibniz in the eighteenth century. He argues that God can think up an infinite number of possible worlds, of which our actual world is just one. Since God is perfect, good, and rational, the actual world he has chosen to create must be the best of all possible worlds. Philosophers of the twentieth century, such as Saul Kripke (1972) and David Lewis (1973), rediscover possible worlds and use it to speak of the truth-value of hypothetical statements and situations. For example, a sentence such as "The King of the United States of America has breakfast" would be considered false. In our world, that is, the twenty-first century, the United States has a president, not a king. However, the sentence could be true if the circumstances were different. If the United States were a kingdom, the sentence would be perfectly fine. In that alternate possible world, the statement would have been true. As this example illustrates, Possible Worlds Theory was initially concerned with the sentence level and whether statements are true or false. Nevertheless, literary theorists have adopted and adapted the theory to discuss aspects of narratives. They considered a text to be a series of worlds. At first, research focused on the possibility and actuality of literary worlds. Are the worlds in, say, *Pride and Prejudice*, a textual actual world, or possible alternate worlds? Later, Possible Worlds Theory was especially applied to genre analysis and the nature of fiction (Ronen 1994; Ryan 1998), and more recently, the narratological structure of games (Punday 2005) and digital fiction (Bell 2010). The last two examples play, by definition, with the idea of multiple possible worlds.

Related Features in Biblical Studies

Possible worlds are about storytelling. Hence, most literary approaches of the Bible touch upon them, although without using the terminology. The basic premise of such studies is the fact that the biblical text is a story, told in various forms, with a religious message. As a result, it can be studied as other stories (or literature more general), many of which happen to be fictional. Like these tales, the Bible invites readers to access the worlds created in the text: worlds of the past as well as of the future, and worlds of dreams, prophecies, and visions.

The first category, of past and future worlds, plays a role in discussions about **plot** and the use of time in biblical texts. Terms such as **flashback**, **prolepsis**, and **chronology** can be found in these discussions. For example, when God speaks to Ezekiel in chapter 5, he not only tells the prophet what to do in the immediate future (shave off hair and beard), but he also takes him back to the past (when Jerusalem was God's chosen one, but she rebelled against him) as well as to the future (judgment will come). All three of these worlds are possible worlds, alternatives to the textual actual world in which God is speaking to Ezekiel. Literary scholarship would call the second world a flashback and the third world a flashforward. Possible Worlds Theory focuses more on the plurality of worlds and their possibility than on the play with time and chronology in the plot. It adds a new dimension that is interested in textual worlds as wholes, rather than in some of their constituents, such as time or place.

Second, possible worlds show affinity with the worlds of dreams, prophecies, and visions in the Bible. These are, first and foremost, treated as subcategories with specific features. A prophecy, for example, requires a prophet delivering a message from God to the people. It includes particular vocabulary, formats, and so on. Some prophecies are further categorized based on their content. Think of the infamous "Oracles against the Nations," which appear in many of the major and minor prophets. Yet, prophecies, as well as dreams and visions, are not just subcategories set apart in the larger narrative of the Bible; they are perceived as set apart because they create possible rather than actual worlds. Note that this effect is the strongest in a first-time reading of the text, especially with texts that include a realization of the dream or prophecy in the textual actual world afterward. For example, when Abram is promised a son in Genesis in a vision, this possible world is actualized later in the textual actual world of the narrative.

One type of texts that deserves attention here are *apocalyptic texts*. Whereas many dreams and visions in the Bible move from possible to textual actual world at some point, if not in the text then through an interplay with the reader's discourse world, such is not the case for apocalyptic texts. These texts project a vision of the end of times, which remains hypothetical for all readers. Think of the books of Revelation or Daniel. The worlds created there are truly alternatives to the textual actual world. Interestingly, the discourse world will, at some points in time (think a war or a pandemic), read these possible worlds as perhaps actual worlds. Once more, the influence of the discourse world is shown here. If this actualization of texts (according to readers) shows anything, it is perhaps the acclaimed universality of literature in general and the Bible in particular. The worlds created are general enough for readers to feel included and specific enough to come across as either real or possibly real.

The Meaning of Possible Worlds in Biblical Studies

The biblical text is a rich text. Possible worlds help to entangle that richness in terms of the worlds created in the text. Think of Joseph in the book of Genesis, who had presumably been eaten by wild animals (37:33), whereas such a thing had never happened in the textual actual world. Construing such a possible world makes for a more interesting narrative, with the opportunity to both present Jacob's feelings (and the reader's response to that) and place the choice to sell Joseph in perspective. In addition, readers assess the degree of possibility and actuality of worlds created in the text. This evaluation is the result of an interplay with the discourse world, including the actual world of the readers and their knowledge, dreams, beliefs, experiences, and so on. For example, a healthy, middle-class person's reading of the book of Revelation will be quite different from that of a poor one with metastatic cancer. Both of them will identify the possible worlds in John's work, but how exactly they will evaluate these worlds and connect them to the textual actual world as well as their own actual world outside the text, will be highly dependent upon their individual situations.

A good number of stories in the Bible include tricksters and deception of various kinds. Very often these characters and features have been addressed morally. Did Jacob wrongfully become one of the patriarchs by tricking Esau out of his birthright (Gen. 25)? Was Ehud a good judge when he fooled Eglon (Judg. 3)? Why did Peter lie to Jesus three times (Luke 22)? Possible worlds can shed a new light on these scenes approaching them as multiple nonactual worlds. They contribute to what literary theorists have called "the poetics of the plot." Indeed, a trickster makes an interesting story as does a lie or ruse here and there. Whether these worlds are true, which would have been the original concern of possible world theorists, or morally good, which is what biblical scholars tend to be interested in, is left aside. Rather, possible worlds in a stylistic setting are about linguistic markers of these worlds and how these worlds contribute to enriching the world of the text as well as the reading experience of the audience. Possible worlds focus on the Bible's story quality, from an objective as well as a subjective point of view.

Finally, possible worlds help to break open a reader's frame of thought and engage with the biblical worlds more open-mindedly. In the end, Ezekiel's visions are not about the truth of them in the actual world, but about what they mean or can mean to a specific reader in specific circumstances. In other words, possible worlds invite modern-day readers to embrace the text as one full of possibilities. Literary approaches to the Bible have often been accused of disrespecting the religious and historical nature of the texts. A focus on possible worlds in the text redefines this discussion. Rather than replacing one label by another, the biblical text can be read from various perspectives. For one person, the letters of Paul represent religious worlds, whereas for others these are instructional worlds or literary worlds, shared with other letters. Yet, each approach will come across multiple worlds evoked by the text. And each reader will face the question of how to deal with these worlds: how to classify them, how to recognize them, and what to make of them in the end.

Case Study: The Valley of Dry Bones

The prophet Ezekiel has many visions throughout the biblical book named after him. In chapter 37, the famous vision of the Valley of Dry Bones takes place. In the textual actual world, Ezekiel has a vision of skeletons. In this alternative world, called a possible world, God orders Ezekiel to prophesy to the bones to come alive again.

> [7] And I prophesied as I had been commanded. And while I was prophesying, there was a sound, and behold, a rattling, and the bones came together, bone to its bone. [8] And I looked, and behold, there were sinews on them, and flesh had come upon them, and skin had covered them, but there was no breath in them. . . . [9] And he said to me, "Prophesy to the breath, prophesy, O son of man, and say to the breath: 'Thus says the LORD God: Come, O breath, from the four winds, and breathe on these slain, that they may live.'" [10] And I prophesied as he commanded me. And the breath entered them, and they lived and stood on their feet, an immensely great army.[1]

The possible world in which the bones come alive could be identified as a fantasy world. The things happening are magical. In the context of the Bible text, one would perhaps rather use the term "miraculous." Although

---

1. All translations in this chapter are the author's own.

the natural law of life and death seems to be distorted in this possible world, other rules the reader is familiar with seem to apply. The bones make a rattling sound, the resurrected bodies have skeletons, but also sinews, flesh and skin, and you need breath to live. In other words, the possible world of the vision is *accessible* to the reader. It is clearly different from the actual world of Ezekiel, as well as from the actual world of the reader, but despite this difference it is close enough to the reader to access the created world and evaluate it as possibility.

What is more, because Ezekiel is speaking as a first-person narrator, he assists the reader in accessing the possible world of the vision. The "I" of Ezekiel is very close to the "I" of the reader, meaning that it requires little effort for the reader to re-center from their actual world, in which bones cannot be resurrected, to a world in which such a process is possible. Another element that plays a role in the reader's ease to re-center is the presence of participants in the vision who exist in the textual actual world as well. Ezekiel and God seem to have no problem whatsoever to step from one world into the other. Their presence in the possible world of the vision makes this world more acceptable. In addition, God's appearance in this alternate world indirectly underscores God's ubiquity to the reader.

In other words, Possible Worlds Theory not only shows us how the text of Ezekiel invites readers to imagine other worlds besides the actual world, and why we, as readers, accept these worlds and classify them as visions rather than as actual world; the theory also reveals that the character of God plays a role in rendering these alternate worlds reliable and accessible to readers.

Ideas for Discussion

1. The book of Esther is an excellent example of a trickster story. Queen Esther helps her people in the most unusual ways. Her antagonists are led astray, imagining worlds that will never become true, in order for the desired plot outcome to be realized. Consider the following two passages:

> Passage 1: Esther 6:4–10: The king is receiving Haman the day after they had both been invited to a dinner by Esther. This event had made Haman feel confident and important.

> Passage 2: Esther 7:7–10: Esther reveals the identity of the enemy to the king.

Identify for both passages the textual actual world and the possible world(s). Which kind of possible world do the texts create? What kind of opportunities do the possible worlds offer in terms of storytelling? Imagine for that matter the story to be told without the possible world. How would you assess the story in terms of emotional response from you as a reader, involvement, interest, and remembering the story?

2. The book of Esther is one of the very few biblical books in which the character God is absent. How would you evaluate this absence in light of the observations you made above about the role of possible worlds in the story? Can you comment on the previously made observation for the example from the book of Ezekiel, where the character God seemed to be present in all worlds of the text, actual and possible?

3. Read Matthew 17:1-8. Distinguish between textual actual world and possible world. Evaluate the accessibility of the possible world (think of time, objects, natural laws, and language). Which elements in the text prompt you to speak of a possible rather than an actual world? What kind of possible world is it? You can consider the perspectives of the different characters in the story. In what respect does the inclusion of this possible world enrich your experience as a reader?

Further Reading

A good introductory piece is "Possible Worlds Theory" in *Key Terms in Stylistics* by Nina Nørgaard, Beatrix Busse, and Rocío Montoro (2010, 139-42). In an accessible way, they explain the basic premises of the approach as well as its use and applicability for the stylistic study of text. Another informative article is Elena Semino's "Possible Worlds: Stylistic Applications" (2005).

The basis of Possible Worlds Theory was first outlined by Gottfried Leibniz in *Essais de Théodicée sur la bonté de Dieu, la liberté de l'homme et l'origine du mal* (1710). His ideas were further developed in later philosophical work, among others, by Saul Kripke, *Naming and Necessity* (1972), and David Lewis, *Counterfactuals* (1973).

Among literary approaches, the most noteworthy work is that of Marie-Laure Ryan. Important pieces are *Possible Worlds, Artificial Intelligence and Narrative Theory* (1991); "Possible Worlds in Recent Literary Theory" (1992); "The Text as World versus the Text as Game: Possible Worlds Semantics and Postmodern Theory" (1998); and "From Parallel Universes to Possible Worlds: Ontological Pluralism in Physics, Narratology and Narrative" (2006). Other work has been done by Thomas G. Pavel, *Fictional Worlds* (1986); Lubomír Doležel, "Mimesis and Possible Worlds" (1988); Ruth Ronen, *Possible Worlds in Literary Theory* (1994); and Elena Semino, *Language and World Creation in Poems and Other Texts* (1997). Recent applications of Possible Word Theory are Daniel Punday, "Creative Accounting: Role-playing Games, Possible-Worlds Theory, and the Agency of Imagination" (2005); and Alice Bell, *The Possible Worlds of Hypertext Fiction* (2010).

There are a good number of introductions to literary analyses of the Bible. The following have separate chapters on time: Shimon Bar-Efrat, *Narrative Art in the Bible* (1989, 141–96); Jan P. Fokkelman, *Reading Biblical Narrative: An Introductory Guide* (1999, 97–111); Daniel Marguerat and Yvan Bourquin, *How to Read Bible Stories* (1999, 85–101); and Yairah Amit, *Reading Biblical Narratives: Literary Criticism and the Hebrew Bible* (2001, 103–14).

Tricksters and deception are analyzed in Susan Niditch, *Underdogs and Tricksters: A Prelude to Biblical Folklore* ([1987] 2000); Cheryl Exum and Johanna W. H. Bos, *Reasoning with the Foxes: Female Wit in a World of Male Power* (1988); and John E. Anderson, *Jacob and the Divine Trickster: A Theology of Deception and YHWH's Fidelity to the Ancestral Promise in the Jacob Cycle* (2011).

Finally, for studies on apocalyptic texts, see, among others, Gerbern Oegema, *Apocalyptic Interpretation of the Bible: Apocalypticism and Biblical Interpretation in Early Judaism, the Apostle Paul, the Historical Jesus and Their Reception History* (2012), and John Collins, *The Oxford Handbook on Apocalyptic Literature* (2014).

Those interested in applications of Possible Worlds Theory to biblical texts can also consult Kobus Marais, "Is This Story Possible? Exploring Possible Worlds Theory" (2007); Mark Brummitt, "Troubling Utopias: Possible Worlds and Possible Voices in the Book of Jeremiah" (2011); and Frauke Uhlenbruch, Anna Angelini, and Anne-Sophie Augier, *Not in the Spaces We Know: An Exploration of Science Fiction and the Bible* (2017).

Relevant sources on Ezekiel and possible worlds are Dereck M. Dascke, "Desolate among Them: Loss, Fantasy, and Recovery in the Book of Ezekiel" (1999), and Frauke Uhlenbruch, *The Nowhere Bible: Utopia, Distopia, Science* (2015).

TWELVE

Reading as Process

Building Text Worlds

Welcome to My World

When the last page of *Harry Potter and the Sorcerer's Stone* is turned, when the lights go up after a stunning performance of *Hamilton* or *A Midsummer Night's Dream*, there can be a sense of swimming back to the surface of everyday life after being submerged in a time and place quite different from one's own. The characters may seem more real than the friend who has been sitting at an arm's length all along. What the author and playwright share in common is not only the ability to create a new time and place filled with intriguing characters and rollicking action; they are also able to draw us into the new setting, engaging our creativity and imagination, often by the way they use theirs. At times, the line between the world of the text or film and the **discourse world** of the reader or viewer becomes fuzzy. *Harry Potter* readers may choose a house to belong to, for example, and recreate the action with friends in real time. Similarly, readers of the biblical text also engage in creating and participating in various **text worlds**. As we read or listen, the world of the text draws us into times and places quite different from our own: ancient Israel and Babylon, floods and pharaohs, chariots and crosses and women in baskets . . . Text World Theory offers a principled way to examine the text itself to discover what clues the author "had in mind" and to thoughtfully interact with the world of the text.

All about Text Worlds

Text worlds are representations of how we process language as we speak or read. According to Joanna Gavins, "We construct mental representations, or **text-worlds**, which enable us to conceptualise and understand every piece of language we encounter" (2007, 2). In other words, we construct mental representations in processing all sorts of communication, from reading to watching films and performances, to looking at billboards, and advertisements.

While text worlds may be generated by written texts, films, and advertisements, this section will talk specifically about written texts. This way of looking at texts intersects with stylistics as it provides a framework for "a principled explanation of the way in which we might keep track of narrative information as we read" (Jeffries and McIntyre 2010, 156). Constructing mental representation as we track through a text is a fascinating idea, an idea that pushes the text and the reader together in the process of making meaning. It raises questions such as: What is the gist of a given text? Which things stick out? Which things are memorable? What parts seem to be forgotten quickly? What does the author want us to know and *how* do they want us to know it? In this way a text-world reading is more than simply collecting and categorizing various aspects of the text in a straight up linguistic or stylistic analysis, but rather it examines the way that the reader and the text interact. The reader brings aspects of the discourse world to bear upon the text and the text guides and constrains meaning production.

Text Worlds Described

A Text World Theory approach can be taken as a general framework for text analysis. According to Jeffries and McIntyre, Text World Theory offers a principled explanation of the way in which we might keep track of narrative information as we read (Jeffries and McIntyre 2010). A text-world approach tracks both world builders, such as time, location, characters and objects, and function advancers, such as material and relational processes. There can be several subworlds involved and moving between worlds is indicated by world switch terms. Mental Spaces Theory lines up well with the idea of creating, structuring, and linking text-worlds and subworlds (see chapter 7). To this discussion, Joanna Gavins adds the concept of double vision, which has to do with "the position that metaphors and their resultant blends take in the discourse as a whole" (Gavins 2007, 152). Gavins's take on double vision is particularly compelling as it allows for a rich explanation of the function of both literary and conceptual metaphors that occur within a complex text. It is also another example of conceptual blending (see chapter 7). Thus, Text World Theory provides readers with tools to identify and describe key features of an extended text and the ability to identify the impact of these features on the message of the text.

Genesis 1:1–5: Building a World—World Builders

Examining Genesis 1:1–5 through the lens of Text World Theory is a useful exercise. As a first step, let us take a detailed look at linguistic elements that may be used to create, connect, and track elements of the text as we read. As mentioned, these are broadly categorized as world builders, function advancers, and indicators of a world switch. These are functional categories and a look at table 12.1 demonstrates that each category comprises more than one type of grammatical form or construction.

Table 12.1 *How to build a world*

How to Build a World
A. World-building elements
1. Time: tense and aspect of verb phrases, temporal phrases
2. Location: adverbials and noun phrases specifying place
3. Characters: proper nouns and pronouns
4. Objects: nouns and pronouns
B. Function-advancing propositions
1. Material processes: intentional or event processes, marked with a downward arrow
2. Relational processes: possessive and circumstantial processes, marked with a horizontal arrow
3. Mental processes: thinking, seeing, hearing, knowing, believing
C. World-switch possibilities
1. Deictic world switch: a shift based upon changes in time and location, i.e. a flash back or projection into the future (These involve a shift in point of view)
2. Attitudinal world switch: a shift based upon expressions of will, wish, or desire (boulomaic modality); a shift based on belief, or purpose (deontic modality)
3. Epistemic world switch: possibility, probability, or hypothetical

There are three basic categories: world-building elements; function-advancing propositions; and world-switching terms. Note that various grammatical forms and constructions are present within each category. First, world builders are generally "nouny" grammatical elements, such as nouns, pronouns and adjectives that indicate time, location, characters and objects. Accounting for these elements is part of almost any close reading. Secondly, function advancers are generally "verby" grammatical elements, such as tense, voice, and mood in Greek. Most importantly, Text World Theory distinguishes between material processes, such as those that are indicated by action verbs, and relational processes that are indicated by verbless clauses, predicate adjectives (and the predicate nominative in Greek). This is a new category that is not generally seen in close reading methodologies and it is one of the most helpful categories for understanding the function of tense, voice, and mood, as well as predicate adjectives and predicate nominatives to students of Greek. Finally, world-switch possibilities are indicated by "little words," such as prepositions and particles, by perception and cognition terms, and by linguistic markers such as the subjunctive case in Greek. While many will read the text in English, or in their first language, there are many ways for nonbiblical languages readers to access the aforementioned information in both online and biblical studies software packages, so it is useful to engage with the concepts as time and interest allow.

These categories are used to explore the text of Genesis 1:1–5 in the tables below.[1]

World builders discovered in the text are laid out in the top box in table 12.2. According to the text, the time notation is "in the beginning." The location is nonspecific, so it is noted as "somewhere in the universe." The only character mentioned is God. This begs the question of who originally observed the action—however, the text is crisp and moves along before we might have time to ponder that question. The objects mentioned in these verses are heaven and earth, light and darkness, day and night.

World building begins with the phrase "In the beginning" in Genesis 1:1. This rather amorphous time margin is possibly one of the most recognizable world builders to be found in the biblical text. It is accompanied by an initial lack of location information as well. The "somewhere out there" aspect of the sentence allows our imaginations to soar. God created the heavens and the earth—truly vast locations. Genesis 1:2 provides an equally amorphous description of the condition of the earth as "formless" and of the waters as nearly invisible, yet windswept. All three statements in Genesis 1:2 are descriptive of the situation and are marked with horizontal arrows that note that the statements are relational.

1. All translations in this chapter are taken from the NRSV.

Table 12.2 *Genesis 1:1–3*

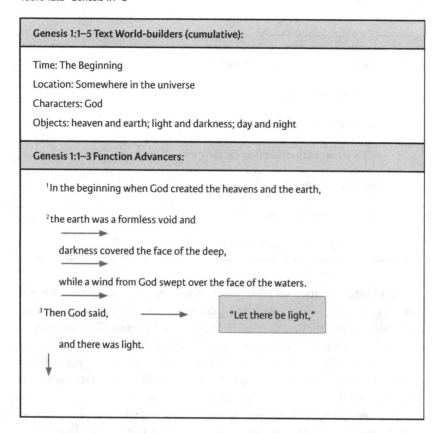

Genesis 1:3–5: Moving the Story Forward

In Genesis 1:3, we see a world switch based upon the semantics of the verb in "and God said." This opens a familiar type of subworld, that of reported speech. (This overlaps with the discussion of verbs of speaking as space builders in Mental Spaces Theory—see chapter 7.) After the short section of reported speech, attention returns to the narrative, which contains a series of material processes:

Table 12.3 *Genesis 1:3–5*

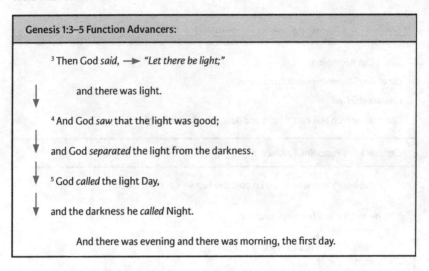

Genesis 1:3–5 Function Advancers:
³ Then God *said,* ──▶ *"Let there be light;"*
and there was light.
⁴ And God *saw* that the light was good;
and God *separated* the light from the darkness.
⁵ God *called* the light Day,
and the darkness he *called* Night.
And there was evening and there was morning, the first day.

Each of the narrative verbal forms in these sentences represents an event process (God "said," "saw," "separated," "called"). The sentences move the narrative forward and they are marked with downward arrows. The statement in verse 4, "and God saw that the light was good," could also be considered a world switch, specifically an attitudinal world switch, where the new space contains God's evaluation of the situation (see table 12.1). This is important because it gives us immediate access to God's own attitude about the situation.

What we end up with is a sort of "discourse analysis light" that includes verbal form analysis and awareness of cognitive spaces that are based upon semantic domains (speech and perception verbs in particular) and other grammatical features. As such, it represents a multifaced, yet principled analysis of the text and the story in the text. Text worlds and mental spaces are two instances of a similar cognitive process, with text worlds being described in a more granular way than mental spaces in many instances. It is useful to hold them together when considering analyzing a text.

Short History

Text World Theory was the brainchild of Paul Werth, who developed the theory in the late 1980s and early 1990s. Werth's goal was to come up with a methodological approach to account for the cognitive processes involved in both the production and interpretation of all forms of communication, texts included. He wrote several articles, including the delightful "How to Build a World (in a Lot Less Than Six Days, Using Only What's in Your Head)" (1995), which lays out many aspects of the theory. Unfortunately, Werth's untimely death in 1995 left a great deal of work to be done, including the editing and publication of his volume *Text Worlds: Representing Conceptual Space in Discourse* (1999), which was accomplished by his colleague Mick Short. It was only a little while before Joanna Gavins became intrigued with Werth's project. Since then she has done extensive work to make Werth's publications available through special collections at the University of Sheffield. Additionally, she has further developed the theory and her volume *Text World Theory: An Introduction* (2007) provides an accessible entry point for those who wish to engage with this way of reading. Vermeulen and Hayes have jumped the divide and continue to explore some of the many ways that Text World Theory can enrich a reading of the biblical text.

Related Features in Biblical Studies

Text World Theory can bring a new degree of clarity to the process of biblical interpretation. Understanding that interpretation involves discovering and analyzing a text world that is created between reader and biblical text highlights the importance of the intersection of various readerly contexts with the text itself. For this reason, while the text is the object of study, it is equally important to be aware of the interpreter and their own language, culture, personal experience, preunderstandings, and presuppositions—their own **encyclopedic background knowledge** of the world. Awareness of what one brings to the text will allow the reader to temporarily bracket their own presuppositions to see more clearly what the text has to say on its own terms. In turn, the reader will be able to see where the text can bring further clarity and understanding to aspects of their own contexts.

A reader's view of the nature of the text is a primary presupposition for reading biblical text. Some readers will address the text as sacred Scripture, with various views of inspiration, inerrancy, infallibility, historicity, and so on. These presuppositions are often formed in relation to a faith tradition and become an integral part of the reader's worldview. Other readers may address the text primarily from an academic perspective, freely exploring the text as literature, reveling in figures of speech and other literary forms, giving attention to language, historical reference, and cultural influences. And some will do both, viewing the biblical text as inspired literature, a world of text worlds where truth and beauty collide.

THE PROCESS OF READING A TEXT

The Meaning of Text Worlds in Biblical Studies

The process of creating meaning as we read the Bible often involves large swathes of text. The creation accounts in Genesis span two chapters; the Sermon on the Mount is three chapters long. Because this is the case, accounting for grammatical details and meaning construction is a process that includes not only lexical choices and sentence construction but also tracking through many, many sentences and paragraphs, work that falls squarely on the shoulders of the reader. Additionally, reading well means being aware of features in a text that move beyond grammar and syntax, such as metaphor, metonymy, and related literary features. We have seen this process of meaning-making at play with the first paragraphs of Genesis. Let us now explore a longer and slightly more complex text, John 15:1-7

Case Study: Jesus as the Vine

While we are reading the English text, it is good to note that the vine discourse in John 15:1-7 is written in Greek as opposed to the Hebrew of Genesis 1:1-5. The two languages are quite different in some regards and many readers will want to employ a text-world analysis using the original languages at some point. Usefully, however, a text-world analysis is undertaken using the same set of criteria no matter what language is involved. A representational diagram can be created with world builders in the top section and function advancers in the lower section. The same subdivisions can be used for function advancers: relational statements can be represented by horizontal arrows and event statements by downward arrows. As we will see, similar world switches may occur as well. These create shifts in perspective that add depth and complexity to the text and to our mental representations of the text.

John 15:1–7: World Builders in the Vine Discourse

If we scan the text of John 15:1-7 looking for world builders, the categories of time and location are lacking. In a traditional close reading, we would go backward into the previous chapter or chapters looking for indicators of the time and location of the discourse. Leaving that aside for the moment, we discover that there are several characters: I (Jesus); you *pl* (hearers); my Father (God); a vinedresser. There are also several objects: a vine, branches, and fruit. In

Table 12.4 *John 15:1–2*

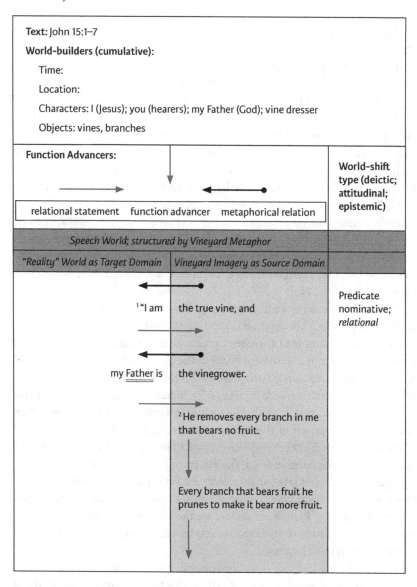

Text: John 15:1–7

World-builders (cumulative):

  Time:

  Location:

  Characters: I (Jesus); you (hearers); my Father (God); vine dresser

  Objects: vines, branches

Function Advancers:	**World-shift type (deictic; attitudinal; epistemic)**
relational statement function advancer metaphorical relation	

Speech World; structured by Vineyard Metaphor

"Reality" World as Target Domain	*Vineyard Imagery as Source Domain*	
[1] "I am	the true vine, and	Predicate nominative; *relational*
my Father is	the vinegrower.	
	[2] He removes every branch in me that bears no fruit.	
	Every branch that bears fruit he prunes to make it bear more fruit.	

the following diagram, a horizontal arrow indicates a relational statement, a vertical arrow indicates a function-advancing statement, and a black arrow indicates a metaphorical statement. Single metaphorical statements straddle

163

the line between the reality world and the metaphorical world, as they participate in both.

The first two statements in John 15:1-7 and the two statements at John 15:5 include imagery based upon references to objects such as vines and branches, a grouping of terms that may be referred to as an image field—an array of images that create a rich picture of a situation. These statements reflect the PEOPLE ARE PLANTS conceptual metaphor and are responsible for an immediate case of what Gavins terms as *double-vision*: the text contains an *extended metaphor* that holds for several verses (see chapter 8). For this reason, the discourse diagram contains one space that represents the reality text world as the **target domain** on the left and the vineyard imagery as the **source domain** on the right to accommodate the extended metaphor. From Gavins's double-vision perspective, when we run into an extended metaphor we retain the initial text world, and the metaphor creates a second world via conceptual blending. She speaks of a *concurrent blended world* and claims that the readers can manage the multiple mental spaces by toggling between them if necessary, which proves to be the case here (Gavins 2007, 152).

The first two statements in John 15:1-7, "I am the true vine" and "my Father is the vine grower," are relational statements using a form of the verb "to be." This is an example of the Greek predicate nominative construction, in which both nouns in a statement occur in the nominative case. In text-world terms, this construction is functionally different from a standard "subject-verb-object/nominative-verb-accusative" sentence. This distinction holds for the English translation as well. The former is a relational predication, often describing some aspect of the subject (horizontal arrow), while the second often describes an event process (downward arrow). John 15:1 provides important background information for the discourse: in this case, Jesus is drawing parallels between his relationship with the Father and the relationship between vine and vinegrower. A pair of similar statements occur at John 15:5, where Jesus states, "I am the vine, you are the branches." These comparisons introduce and continue an extended conceptual metaphor that structures many verses of the discourse.

Each of the activities of the vinegrower is presented as an event process, indicated by the downward facing arrow. The two statements are nearly a parallel, describing the actions of the vinegrower as he removes branches that do not bear fruit and prunes branches that do bear fruit.

Table 12.5 *John 15:3–5*

Reality World	Metaphor World	World Shift
³ You have already been cleansed		**Deictic:** time and space shift
by the word that I have spoken		
⁴ Abide in me		**Attitudinal** (command, imperative verbal form)
	Just as the branch cannot bear	
	fruit by itself unless it abides in the vine,	
neither can you [ ] unless you abide in me.		
⁵ I am	the vine,	
you are	the branches.	
Those who abide in me	bear much fruit	
because apart from me you can do nothing.		**Epistemic:** conditional/ hypothetical

John 15:1–5: World Switching in the Vine Discourse

Meaning making in John 15:1–5 takes place on several levels. First there is the main separation between the reality world (target domain) and the metaphorical world (source domain). Within these two spaces, a number of subworlds arise.

In John 15:3 a deictic time shift opens a past time subworld (see chapter 4). In verse 3, the deictic shift is placed on the reality side of the diagram, as it refers to the disciples as hearers. Here, a wordplay between the Greek term *kathairei* (he prunes) in verse 2 and *katharoi* (cleansed) creates a loose connection between the branches that the Father prunes in the metaphor world and Jesus's assurance that the disciples have already (ēdē) been cleansed by the word he has spoken to them in the reality world.

In John 15:4, the imperative verb, "abide," opens an attitudinal subworld, as the imperative form indicates a command. In verse 4 the attitudinal shift of command is placed on the "reality" side of the diagram, as the imperative "to abide" (meinate) is directed to the hearers. This is followed by a brief toggle between the reference to the fruit-bearing conditions for plants on the one hand and the necessity for remaining or abiding in Jesus on the other hand.

In John 15:5 the second set of relational statements, "I am the vine, you are the branches," leads into a contrastive subworld: Those who abide in Jesus bear much fruit.

In John 15:6 a second contrastive subworld is opened by the phrase "Whoever does not abide" (ean mē tis menē en emoi). This statement shifts the narration to a negative epistemic conditional due to the conditional term "If" (ean). The following series of material processes, indicated by downward arrows, demonstrates the fate that will befall those who do not remain/abide in Jesus. Significantly, the two epistemic conditionals straddle the reality world and the metaphoric world.

In verse 7, the conditional term "If" (ean) in the parallel phrases "If you abide in me and my words abide in you" (ean meinēte en emoi kai ta rhēmata mou en humin meinē) shifts the narration to a positive epistemic conditional. Within this space, there is an embedded space to accommodate the deictic time shift indicated by the future tense of the verb "And it will be done [genēsetai] for you." Verse 7 is the last toggle between the reality world and the metaphor world until verse 16 of the passage, which briefly refers to bearing fruit and wraps up the entire discourse with further references to remaining in Jesus and asking the Father for answers. The double-vision text worlds and the various subworlds create the sense of an intimate and lively discussion, where Jesus encourages his hearers to choose well. He wants them to abide in him and to carry his words inside themselves. The discussion is largely framed by the CONTAINMENT SCHEMA and invites consideration of what it means to be in Christ.

Table 12.6 *John 15:6-7*

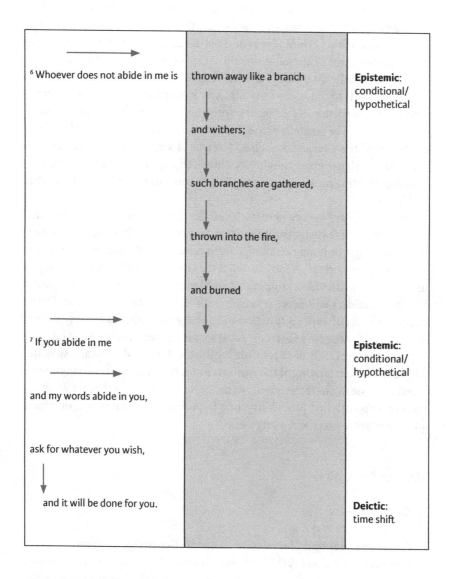

Wrapping It Up

This text-world analysis raises several points to ponder. One of these is the way that vineyard imagery and resultant conceptual metaphors structure this stretch of text. The first two predicate nominatives at 15:1 are indicative of the relationship between Jesus and the Father; the second at 15:5 are indicative of the relationship between Jesus and his disciples. Jesus, the Vine, stands at the center point of the relationship complex. It seems that by including both Jesus and the disciples as an interrelated vine and branches entity, the metaphor shifts to the SOCIETY IS A PLANT metaphor (see chapter 8), which fits very well with the discussion of positive and negative fruit-bearing behaviors discussed. The position of the Father as vinegrower gives him the role of the tender of the vine and branches. The role of vinegrower falls to an entity presented as higher up on the animacy hierarchy than the vine and branches, thus highlighting his superintending role in contrast to the less animate vine and branches.

Text worlds are everywhere in the biblical text and using the text-world model can provide insights into the text that may enrich and expand established readings, or it may encourage fresh readings that engage with the various aspects of the text. A look through the "How to Build a World" synopsis in table 12.1 will provide a jumping off point for further study. Combing a text for world builders will develop facility with the analysis of grammar. Determining aspects of various function-advancing propositions will encourage fine-tuning the cognitive basis of verbal forms and lexical choices. And, perhaps most importantly of all, examining the text for world shifts and switches will refine understanding of the various contexts represented in a single text: location, time, a character's will, wish, or desire, and whether a statement represents possibility, probability, or a hypothetical situation—all of which are important aspects of reading well.

Ideas for Discussion

Genesis 1:1–2:2

1. Continue exploring the initial creation story in Genesis by taking turns reading Genesis 1:1–2:2 aloud. While one person reads, have another person sketch what they are hearing. Compare the drawings. Are the drawings alike or different? Did each person draw a single detailed picture, or did they draw several small individual pictures?
2. Read Genesis 1:1–2:2 again, taking time to note the presence of world builders. Record references to time, location, characters, and objects. What characters

are present throughout the chapter? What new characters are added? Which of the characters does the most speaking?

3. Finally, think about the presence of repetitions such as "God said" and "And there was evening and there was morning." How does the world-building phrase "and God said" function within the text? How about the phrase "And there was evening and there was morning"? What does this exercise tell us about how we hear and conceptualize the text?

Contextualizing John 15:1–7

The longer text-world analysis example of John 15:1–7 is a discourse, a conversation between Jesus and his followers. Because the section was abstracted from the longer text, we noted that there were no time or location world builders for the conversation; we do not know where it took place, or when. This leaves questions, and one way to address them is to look at the surrounding text for clues. Another way to address these questions is to turn to commentaries or other reference books.

1. First, take some time to read John 13 and 14. What time or location clues are found in these chapters? Do these chapters help to set the discourse in its larger context? Why or why not?
2. Secondly, find a commentary or other reference book and look up what that author has to say about the time and location of the discourse. Does this information add to what you have discovered by reading around in the text? Why or why not?
3. Finally, how does an understanding of the time and location of the discourse add meaning to what we discussed in the text-world account?

Further Reading

For a winsome and detailed introduction to Text World Theory, see Paul Werth's seminal essay, "How to Build a World (in a Lot Less Than Six Days, Using Only What's in Your Head)" (1995). The intrepid reader may wish to follow this by Werth's more detailed presentation in *Text Worlds: Representing Conceptual Space in Discourse* (1999). For practical applications of Text World Theory, see Joanna Gavins's volume *Text World Theory: An Introduc-*

tion (2007). Lesley Jeffries and Dan McIntyre include a section on Text World Theory in their volume, *Stylistics* (2010).

Those who are interested in discourse analysis will benefit from the explanations in Robert E. Longacre, *The Grammar of Discourse* (1983).

Glossary

The references in parentheses indicate chapters in which the terms are discussed in depth.

acrostic: A poem in which the first letters of each line or phrase spell out a word or sentence. In the case of an alphabetic acrostic, those beginning letters make up the alphabet. (1)

actual world (AW): Or real world, in which we live; one of a number of possible worlds. (11)

alliteration: A stylistic device in which words with the same (often initial) consonant follow one another. Also defined as a sound effect of certain wordplay types. (3, 9)

alternate textual (possible) world (APW): An alternative to the textual actual world, that is, the world identified as real in the text. (11)

analogy: A comparison between two (or more) elements with similar features. (6)

background style: A style of writing that leaves a lot of gaps. (3)

bottom-up: *See* "projection."

caricature: Body parts of a character are singled out to represent the whole being. (9)

chiasm: A literary device in which parts A and B of a sentence appear in reversed order in the next sentence, thus as B and A. (1, 3, 10)

chronology: The order of events according to the time they occurred. (11)

coherence: The state of forming a whole and being perceived in that way. (9)

construal: The way we think about a given situation, including ideas such as perspective, location, scale, and point of view. (4, 5)

construction: A top-down process, where a reader brings pre-existing knowledge to the text to understand it. (6)

context: That which is surrounding the text. This can be other stories from the same cultural realm, but also the historical setting or, more broadly, knowledge that is relevant to understand the text. (6)

counterpart: A representation of an entity in an alternate world at a different point in time, for example, Jerusalem mentioned in a prophecy in the past, present, and future. (11)

counterreading: A reading of the text that consciously goes against the unconscious process of integrating the discourse world of writer and reader. (10)

defamiliarization: The effect on readers when familiar structures, such as word order or standard language, are disrupted by the use of a different word order or a literary device. When readers come across something unfamiliar, they will look at it more carefully. (3)

deictic center: The speaking character whose location in time and space determines how a situation is viewed. (4)

deixis: Terms and constructions that indicate location in time and space, usually determined by the relationship of these elements with a speaking character, determined by the narrator. (4, 5)

discourse world: The immediate situational context surrounding the reading of a text. (introduction, 4, 10, 12)

discourse world (split): The situation in which the immediate situational context surrounding the reading of a text is different for the reader and the author. (introduction, 10)

encyclopedic background knowledge: Stored knowledge in a reader's mind including factual knowledge, emotions, thoughts, and feelings. (1, 12)

figure: The object, that which draws attention (introduction, 3)

flashback: An interruption of the chronology of a story to go back to a moment in the past. (11)

foreground style: A style of writing that is very detailed. (3)

foregrounding: The act of emphasizing a specific element in a narrative, for example, by repeating it frequently or by changing the standard word order of a sentence. (3)

frame knowledge, frame: A recognizable organization of elements and relations which is present in long-term memory and available to short-term memory when making meaning while reading, thinking, and talking. (7)

function advancers: Propositions that catch the action in a text world, often with verbal forms. The main groups are material processes (with verbs such as "come") and relational processes (with the verb "to be"). (12)

gaps: Missing information in the text. (6)

genre: A category of art, music, or literature defined by stylistic features, for example, a prince and a princess for a fairytale, gods for a myth. (1, 2)

ground: Surroundings, background, that which does not draw attention. (introduction, 3, 4)

ICM, Idealized Cognitive Model: Structures of knowledge that rely on relations between categories. Examples are schemas, metaphors, and metonymies. (2, 6)

image schema: Information packages that we depend on at the subconscious level for many aspects of daily life. CONTAINMENT and SOURCE-PATH-GOAL are two common image schemas. (5)

immersion: A process in which a reader after having merged his perspective with that of the text experiences a feeling of being integrated into the text world. (11)

impossible world: A world that violates its own rules. (11)

incrementation: Knowledge moving from the private to the public, shared sphere of two or more participants in a discourse. (10)

intertextuality: The relationship between different texts. (2)

lexeme: A basic unit of meaning in a given language, which can be a word or group of words. (1)

lexical domain: Also called lexical group, a group of words that are derived from the same lexical root and therefore have a shared meaning base. For example, dog-dogging-doggedly. (1)

markedness: Opposite of not being marked or default option. In linguistics this refers, for example, to word order. The standard word order is unmarked, drawing no attention. A deviation, however, does, hence the term "marked word order." (2)

metaphor (conceptual): Understanding one conceptual domain in terms of another, for example, time in terms of money. (1, 6, 9)

metaphor (literary or novel metaphor): A literary device in which an unusual image is used to talk about something else. Contrary to conceptual metaphors, literary metaphors (also called novel metaphors) do not draw on well-known connections between, for example, happiness and a state of well-being. On the contrary, they explore connections that have not been made before, which is exactly why they draw readers' attention. (introduction, 3, 8)

metonymic agency: When body parts replace a person and become actors, for example, "the hand of God." (9)

metonymy (conceptual): Understanding one category in terms of another within one conceptual domain, for example, a place for an institution (located at that place). (introduction, 6, 9)

metonymy (literary or novel): A figure of speech in which one item is replaced by another that is related to it. For example, a part for a whole. Note that a literary metonymy differs from a conceptual one in that it is unusual and stands out in the text, whereas a conceptual metonymy often goes unnoticed. (1)

modality: The mode in which something appears (aural, visual, written, performed, etc.). (2)

parallelism: A mode of composition in which sentences have corresponding constructions and/or content. For example, if a sentence has the construction AB, the subsequent parallel line will also have AB as structure. Parallelism is typical of biblical poetry. (1, 2, 3, 9, 10)

personification: A type of metaphor in which an entity is compared to a person, for example GOD IS A PERSON. (7, 9)

perspective: Presenting the subjective point of view of a character in text. (introduction, 4)

plot: The story in the order as it is told in a book (thus, with flashbacks and so on). (11)

polysemy: The feature of some words to have more than one meaning. (2)

possible world: An alternative to the real or actual world. (introduction, 11)

principle of minimal departure: The assumption of readers that what they are reading is close to what they know. (11)

projection: A bottom-up process where the reader draws meaning from the text. (6)

prolepsis: A flashforward, an interruption of the chronology of a story to a moment in the future. (11)

prototype: The best example of a category, forms the basis of classification, and forms a reference point for further classification of new examples of the category. (2)

radial structure: Representation of categories with the best example (prototype) in the middle and other examples around it. The closer the example is to the central example, the better it represents the category. (2)

re-centering: A process where the reader replaces his own actual world as the starting point and adopts the textual actual world (or a possible world) as the starting point. (11)

reported speech: When you tell someone what someone else has said. Also called indirect speech. For example: She said that this is a great book. (12)

root: Three letter base in Biblical Hebrew to which elements are added in order to turn the root (a theoretical construct) into an actual word one would use. For example, the root *m-l-k* would result in words such as *melek* (king) and *malak* (he ruled). (1)

schema: A structured bit of context or background knowledge a reader relies on and that is triggered by the text, also called a script or scenario, for example a DELIVERANCE schema or a SUPPER schema. (introduction, 5, 6)

semantic domain: A group of words that are semantically related; an area of meaning and the words used to talk about it. For example, the semantic domain of rulership includes words such as "king" and "kingdom" (both lexically related) but also "rule," "govern," and "lead." (1)

semiotic triangle: A visualization of the three elements present in a linguistic sign: the form, the content, and the referent. (9)

simile: A comparison of two things using the words "like" or "as." For example, "your eyes are like doves" (Song 1:15). (3)

source: Vehicle entity, the category (for metonymy) or the domain (for metaphor) you compare to another category or domain. For example, in the metonymy ARK FOR GOD, the ark is the source, and in the metaphor TIME IS MONEY, money is the source. (8, 9, 12)

stylistic figures: Formal interventions of writers to the language of a text in order to, among others, draw readers' attention. Typical examples are alliteration, chiasm, and novel metaphor. (3, 9)

subworld: Or world switch, a shift in time, location, or modality that brings the reader to create a new text world with parameters (time, location, objects, characters) different from the initial text world. (12)

synecdoche: A subtype of metonymy, traditionally used for the subtype PART FOR WHOLE and WHOLE FOR PART. (11)

target: Target entity, the category (for metonymy) or the domain (for metaphor) you compare another category or domain to. For example, in the metonymy ARK FOR GOD, God is the target, and in the metaphor TIME IS MONEY, time is the target. (8, 9, 12)

textual actual world (TAW): The actual world of the text, the world identified as real in the text. (11)

text worlds: Mental representations to understand human discourse. Typical attributes are time, place, enactors (characters), and objects that build up the world. In addition, verbal forms can give background knowledge or move the story forward. (introduction, 4, 12)

top-down: See "construction."

type-scene: A scene that draws on a specific set of actions, participants, and objects, for example, a betrothal scene, such as in Genesis 24. (6)

viewpoint: The eyes we see through according to the text, particularly regarding a character's perspective. (introduction, 4)

world builders: References to time, location, characters, and objects that build up the text world. (12)

world switch: See subworld. (12)

Bibliography

Al-Sharafi, Abdul. 2004. *Textual Metonymy: A Semiotic Approach*. London: Casell.

Alter, Robert. 1980. *The Art of Biblical Narrative*. New York: Basic Books.

———. 1985. *The Art of Biblical Poetry*. New York: Basic Books.

———. 2011. *The Art of Biblical Narrative*. Rev. and updated ed. New York: Basic Books.

Alter, Robert, and Frank Kermode, eds. 1978. *The Literary Guide to the Bible*. Cambridge: Harvard University Press.

Amit, Yairah. 2001. *Reading Biblical Narratives: Literary Criticism and the Hebrew Bible*. Minneapolis: Fortress.

Anderson, John E. 2011. *Jacob and the Divine Trickster: A Theology of Deception and YHWH's Fidelity to the Ancestral Promise in the Jacob Cycle*. Siphrut 5. Winona Lake, IN: Eisenbrauns.

Anderson, Richard C., and P. David Pearson. 1984. "A Schema-Theoretic View of Basic Processes in Reading Comprehension." Pages 255–91 in *Handbook of Reading Research*. Edited by P. David Pearson. New York: Longman.

Arata, Luigi. 2005. "The Definition of Metonymy in Ancient Greece." *Style* 39, no. 1: 55–70.

Arnheim, Rudolf. 1957. *Art and Visual Perception*. London: Faber & Faber.

Assis, Elie. 2009. *Flashes of Fire: A Literary Analysis of the Song of Songs*. New York: Bloomsbury.

Auerbach, Erich. 1946. *Mimesis: Dargestellte Wirklichkeit in der abenländischen Literatur*. Bern: A. Francke Ag. Verlag.

Barcelona, Antonio. 2007. "The Role of Metonymy in Meaning Construction at a Discourse Level." Pages 51–75 in *Aspects of Meaning Construction*. Edited by Günter Radden, Klaus-Michael Köpcke, Thomas Berg, and Peter Siemund. London: John Benjamins.

Bar-Efrat, Shimon. 1989. *Narrative Art in the Bible*. Sheffield: Almond.

Bartlett, Frederic C. 1932. *Remembering: A Study in Experimental and Social Psychology*. Repr. 1995. Cambridge: Cambridge University Press.

Barton, John, ed. 2016. *The Hebrew Bible: A Critical Companion*. Princeton: Princeton University Press.

———. 2019. *The Bible: The Basics*. New York: Routledge.

Beardslee, David C., and Max Wertheimer, eds. 1958. *Readings in Perception*. Princeton, NJ: Van Nostrand.

Bell, Alice. 2010. *The Possible Worlds of Hypertext Fiction*. Basingstoke, UK: Palgrave Macmillan.

Ben Zvi, Ehud. 2003. *Signs of Jonah: Reading and Rereading in Ancient Yehud*. JSOTSup 367. London: Sheffield Academic Press.

Bergen, Robert D. 1994. *Biblical Hebrew and Discourse Linguistics*. Dallas: Summer Institute of Linguistics.

Berlin, Adele. 1983. *Poetics and Interpretation of Biblical Narrative*. Sheffield: Almond.

———. 2008. *The Dynamics of Biblical Parallelism*. Rev. and expanded ed. Grand Rapids: Eerdmans.

Blank, Andreas. 1999. "Co-presence and Succession: A Cognitive Typology of Metonymy." Pages 169–91 in *Metonymy in Language and Thought*. Edited by Klaus-Uwe Panther and Günter Radden. Amsterdam: John Benjamins.

Boxall, Ian. 2019. *Matthew through the Centuries*. Wiley Blackwell Bible Commentaries. Hoboken, NJ: Wiley & Sons.

Brenner, Athalya, and Carole Fontaine, eds. 1997. *A Feminist Companion to Reading the Bible: Approaches, Methods and Strategies*. Sheffield: Sheffield Academic.

Brisard, Frank, ed. 2002. *Grounding: The Epistemic Footing of Deixis and Reference*. Cognitive Linguistics Research 21. Berlin: de Gruyter.

Brown, Raymond E., and Marion Soards. 2016. *An Introduction to the New Testament: The Abridged Edition*. New Haven: Yale University Press.

Broyles, Craig C. 2001. *Interpreting the Old Testament: A Guide for Exegesis*. Grand Rapids: Baker Academic.

Brummitt, Mark. 2011. "Troubling Utopias: Possible Worlds and Possible Voices in the Book of Jeremiah." Pages 175–89 in *Jeremiah (Dis)Placed: New Directions in Writing/Reading Jeremiah*. Edited by A. R. Pete Diamond and Louis Stulman. LHBOTS 527. London: T&T Clark.

Carr, David. 2011. *The Formation of the Hebrew Bible*. Oxford: Oxford University Press.

Carter, Warren. 2000. *Matthew and the Margins: A Socio-Political Reading and Religious Reading*. London/New York: T&T Clark.

Chau, Kevin. 2014. "Metaphor's Forgotten Brother: A Survey of Metonymy in Biblical Hebrew Poetry." *Journal for Semitics* 23, no. 2: 633–52.

Collins, John, ed. 1979. *Apocalypse: The Morphology of a Genre*. Semeia 14.

———, ed. 2014. *The Oxford Handbook on Apocalyptic Literature*. Oxford: Oxford University Press.

Conway, Colleen. 2017. *Sex and Slaughter in the Tent of Jael: A Cultural History of a Biblical Story*. New York: Oxford University Press.

Coogan, Michael. 2009. *A Brief Introduction to the Old Testament: The Hebrew Bible in Its Context*. New York: Oxford University Press.

Cook, Guy. 1994. *Discourse and Literature: The Interplay of Form and Mind*. Oxford: Oxford University Press.

Cotrozzi, Stefano. 2010. *Expect the Unexpected: Aspects of Pragmatic Foregrounding in Old Testament Narrative*. LHBOTS 510. New York: T&T Clark.

Croft, William, and D. A. Cruse. *Cognitive Linguistics*. Cambridge: Cambridge University Press, 2004.

Culpeper, Jonathan. 2001. *Language and Characterisation: People in Plays and Other Texts*. New York: Longman.

Culpepper, Alan R. 1983. *Anatomy of the Fourth Gospel: A Study in Literary Design*. Philadelphia: Fortress.

Dascke, Dereck M. 1999. "Desolate among Them: Loss, Fantasy, and Recovery in the Book of Ezekiel." *American Imago* 56, no. 2: 105–32.

Dawson, David Allan. 1994. *Text-Linguistics and Biblical Hebrew*. JSOTSup 177. Sheffield: Sheffield Academic Press.

Denroche, Charles. 2015. *Metonymy and Language: A New Theory of Linguistic Processing*. New York/London: Routledge.

Doležel, Lubomír. 1988. "Mimesis and Possible Worlds." *Poetics Today* 9, no. 3: 475–97.

Dubois, Carl D. 1999. "Metonymy and Synecdoche in the New Testament." *SIL International Resources* (for translators): 1–127, published as a revision and augmentation of John Beekman, "Metonymy and Synecdoche," *Notes on Translation* 23 (1967): 12–25. http://www.sil.org/resources/archives/47346.

Duvall, J. Scott, and J. Daniel Hays. 2012. *Grasping God's Word: A Hands-on Approach to Reading, Interpreting, and Applying the Bible*. 3rd ed. Grand Rapids: Zondervan.

Exum, Cheryl. 2019. *Art as Biblical Commentary: Visual Criticism from Hagar the Wife of Abraham to Mary the Mother of Jesus*. LHBOTS 694. London/New York: T&T Clark.

Exum, Cheryl, and Johanna W. H. Bos, eds. 1988. *Reasoning with the Foxes: Female Wit in a World of Male Power*. Semeia 42. Atlanta: Scholars Press.

Fauconnier, Gilles. 1994. *Mental Spaces: Aspects of Meaning Construction in Natural Language*. Cambridge: Cambridge University Press.

——. 1997. *Mappings in Thought and Language*. Cambridge: Cambridge University Press.

Fauconnier, Gilles, and Eve Sweetser. 1996. *Spaces, Worlds, and Grammar*. Chicago: University of Chicago Press.

Fauconnier, Gilles, and Mark Turner. 1996. "Blending as a Central Process of Grammar." Pages 113–29 in *Conceptual Structure, Discourse and Language*. Edited by Adele E. Goldberg. Stanford: CSLI.

——. 2002. *The Way We Think: Conceptual Blending and the Mind's Hidden Complexities*. New York: Basic Books.

Fillmore, Charles. 1985. "Frames and the Semantics of Understanding." *Quaderni di Semantica* 6: 222–54.

Fishbane, Michael. 1979. *Biblical Text and Texture: A Literary Reading of Selected Texts*. New York: Schocken Books.

Fokkelman, Jan P. 1999. *Reading Biblical Narrative: An Introductory Guide*. Louisville: Westminster John Knox.

Freeman, Margaret H. 2002. "Cognitive Mapping in Literary Analysis." *Style* 36, no. 3: 1–13.

Fu, Zhengling. 2016. "The Application of Conceptual Metonymy in Discourse Coherence." *International Journal of English Language Education* 4, no. 2: 33–41.

Gavins, Joanna. 2007. *Text World Theory: An Introduction*. Edinburgh: Edinburgh University Press.

Gibbons, Alison, and Sarah Whiteley. 2018. *Contemporary Stylistics: Language, Cognition, Interpretation*. Edinburgh: Edinburgh University Press.

Gibbs, Raymond W. 2006. *Embodiment and Cognitive Science*. Cambridge: Cambridge University Press.

——. 2007. "Experiential Tests of Figurative Meaning Construction." Pages 19–32 in *Aspects of Meaning Construction*. Edited by Günter Radden, Klaus-Michael Köpcke, Thomas Berg, and Peter Siemund. London: John Benjamins.

Giovanelli, Marcello, and Chloe Harrison. 2018. *Cognitive Grammar in Stylistics: A Practical Guide*. London: Bloomsbury.

Green, Keith, ed. 1995. *New Essays in Deixis: Discourse, Narrative, Literature*. Costerus 103. Amsterdam: Rodopi.

Gregoriou, Christiana. 2009. *English Literary Stylistics. Perspectives on the English Language*. Basingstoke, UK/New York: Palgrave Macmillan.

Gunkel, Hermann. (1926) 1967. *The Psalms: A Form-Critical Introduction*. Philadelphia: Fortress.

Gunn, David M., and Danna Nolan Fewell. 1993. *Narrative in the Hebrew Bible.* Oxford: Oxford University Press.

Harrison, Chloe, and Louise Nuttall. 2018. "Re-reading in Stylistics." *Language and Literature* 27, no. 3: 176–95.

Hayes, Elizabeth R. 2007. "The Influence of Ezekiel 37 on 2 Corinthians 6:14–7:1." Pages 115–28 in *The Book of Ezekiel and Its Influence.* Edited by Johannes Tromp and H. J. De Jonge. Hampshire: Ashgate.

———. 2008. *The Pragmatics of Perception and Cognition in MT Jeremiah 1.1–6.30: A Cognitive Linguistics Approach.* Berlin: de Gruyter.

———. 2009. "Of Branches, Pots and Figs: Jeremiah's Visions from a Cognitive Perspective." Pages 89–102 in *Prophecy in the Book of Jeremiah.* Edited by Hans M. Barstad and Reinhard G. Kratz. BZAW. Berlin: de Gruyter.

———. 2012. "The One Who Brings Justice: Conceptualizing the Role of 'the Servant' in Isaiah 42:1–4 and Matthew 12:15–21." Pages 143–51 in *Let Us Go up to Zion: Essays in Honour of H. G. M. Williamson.* Edited by Iain Provan and Mark J. Boda. Supplements to Vetus Testamentum 153. Leiden: Brill.

Hays, Richard B., Stefan Alkier, and Leroy A. Huizenga, eds. 2009. *Reading the Bible Intertextually.* Waco: Baylor University Press.

Heimerdinger, Jean-Marc. 1999. *Topic, Focus and Foreground in Ancient Hebrew Narratives.* JSOTSup 295. Sheffield: Sheffield Academic Press.

Hort, Greta. 1959. "The Plagues of Egypt." *Zeitschrift für Alttestamentliche Wissenschaft* 69, nos. 1–4: 84–103.

Hurowitz, Victor A. 1985. "The Priestly Account of Building the Temple." *Journal of the American Oriental Society* 105, no. 1: 21–30.

Hurtado, Larry. 2014. "Oral Fixation and New Testament Studies? 'Orality,' 'Performance' and Reading Texts in Early Christianity." *New Testament Studies* 60, no. 3: 321–40.

Howe, Bonnie. 2006. *Because You Bear This Name: Conceptual Metaphor and the Moral Meaning of 1 Peter.* Biblical Interpretation Series 81. Leiden: Brill.

James, Elaine T. 2017. *Landscapes of the Song of Songs: Poetry and Place.* New York: Oxford University Press.

Jeffries, Lesley, and Dan McIntyre. 2010. *Stylistics.* Cambridge Textbooks in Linguistics. Cambridge: Cambridge University Press.

Johnson, Mark. 1987. *The Body in the Mind: The Bodily Basis of Meaning, Imagination, and Reason.* Chicago: University of Chicago Press.

Kövecses, Zoltán. 2002. *Metaphor: A Practical Introduction.* Oxford: Oxford University Press.

———. 2010. *Metaphor: A Practical Introduction.* 2nd ed. Oxford: Oxford University Press.

Kövecses, Zoltán, and Bálint Koller. 2006. *Language, Mind, and Culture: A Practical Introduction*. New York: Oxford.

Kripke, Saul. 1972. *Naming and Necessity*. Oxford: Blackwell.

Kugel, James. 1981. *The Idea of Biblical Poetry: Parallelism and Its History*. Baltimore: Johns Hopkins University Press.

Labahn, Antje. 2013. *Conceptual Metaphors in Poetic Texts: Proceedings of the Metaphor Research Group of the European Association of Biblical Studies in Lincoln 2009*. Perspectives on Hebrew Scriptures and Its Contexts 18. Piscataway, NJ: Gorgias.

Lahey, Ernestine. 2005. "Text-World Landscapes and English-Canadian National Identity in the Poetry of Al Purdy, Alden Nowlan, and Milton Acorn." PhD thesis, University of Nottingham.

Lakoff, George. 1987. *Women, Fire and Dangerous Things: What Categories Reveal about the Mind*. Chicago: University of Chicago Press.

Lakoff, George, and Mark Johnson. 1980. *Metaphors We Live By*. Chicago: University of Chicago Press.

———. 1999. *Philosophy in the Flesh: The Embodied Mind and Its Challenge to Western Thought*. New York: Basic Books.

———. 2003. *Metaphors We Live By*. Chicago: University of Chicago Press.

Landau, Brent. 2010. *Revelation of the Magi: The Lost Tale of the Wise Men's Journey to Bethlehem*. New York: HarperOne.

Landy, Francis. 1983. *Paradoxes of Paradise: Identity and Difference in the Song of Songs*. Sheffield: Almond.

Langacker, Ronald W. 1983. *Foundations of Cognitive Grammar*. Bloomington: Indiana University Linguistics Club.

———. 1987. *Foundations of Cognitive Grammar*. Vol. 1: *Theoretical Prerequisites*. Stanford: Stanford University Press.

———. 1999. *Grammar and Conceptualization*. Cognitive Linguistics Research 14. Berlin: de Gruyter.

———. 2001. "Discourse in Cognitive Grammar." *Cognitive Linguistics* 12: 143–88.

———. 2002a. *Concept, Image, and Symbol: The Cognitive Basis of Grammar*. 2nd ed. Cognitive Linguistics Research 1. Berlin: de Gruyter.

———. 2002b. "Deixis and Subjectivity." Pages 1–28 in *Grounding: The Epistemic Footing of Deixis and Reference*. Edited by Frank Brisard. Berlin: de Gruyter.

———. 2003. "Context, Cognition, and Semantics: A Unified Dynamic Approach." Pages 179–230 in *Job 28: Cognition in Context*. Edited by E. J. van Wolde. Leiden: Brill.

Lee, David. 2001. *Cognitive Linguistics: An Introduction*. Oxford: Oxford University Press.

Leibniz, Gottfried. 1710. *Essais de Théodicée sur la bonté de Dieu, la liberté de l'homme et l'origine du mal*. Amsterdam.

Lemmelijn, Benedikte. 2007. "Not Fact, Yet True: Historicity versus Theology in the 'Plague Narrative' (Ex 7-11)." *Old Testament Essays* 20, no. 2: 395-217.

Lewis, David. 1973. *Counterfactuals*. Cambridge: Cambridge University Press.

Lieb, Michael, Emma Mason, and Jonathan Roberts, eds. 2011. *The Oxford Handbook of the Reception History of the Bible*. Oxford: Oxford University Press.

Longacre, Robert E. 1996. *The Grammar of Discourse*. Topics in Language and Linguistics. 2nd ed. New York: Plenum.

———. 2003. *Joseph: A Story of Divine Providence: A Text Theoretical and Textlinguistic Analysis of Genesis 37 and 39-48*. 2nd ed. Winona Lake, IN: Eisenbrauns.

Louw, Johannes P., and Eugene Albert Nida. 1996. Greek-English Lexicon of the New Testament: Based on Semantic Domains. New York: United Bible Societies.

Macky, Peter W. 1990. *The Centrality of Metaphors to Biblical Thought: A Method for Interpreting the Bible*. Lewiston, NY: Mellen.

Marais, Kobus. 2007. "Is This Story Possible? Exploring Possible Worlds Theory." *Old Testament Essays* 20, no. 1: 158-69.

Marguerat, Daniel, and Yvan Bourquin, 1999. *How to Read Bible Stories*. London: SCM.

McCasland, S. Vernon. 1949. "Some New Testament Metonyms for God." *Journal of Biblical Literature* 68, no. 2: 99-113.

McKay, Niall. 2013. "Status Update: The Many Faces of Intertextuality in New Testament Study." *Religion and Theology* 20, nos. 1-2: 84-106.

Meredith, Christopher. 2013. *Journeys in the Songscape: Space and the Song of Songs*. Sheffield: Sheffield Phoenix.

Miller, Geoffrey. 2011. "Intertextuality in Old Testament Research." *Currents in Biblical Research* 9, no. 3: 283-309.

Minsky, Marvin. 1975. "A Framework for Representing Knowledge." Pages 221-77 in *The Psychology of Computer Vision*. Edited by P. E. Winston. New York: McGraw-Hill.

———. 1986. *The Society of Mind*. London: Heinemann.

Nerlich, Brigitte, D. Clarke, and Z. Todd. 1999. "'Mummy, I Like Being a Sandwich': Metonymy in Language Acquisition." Pages 361-83 in *Metonymy in Language and Thought*. Edited by Klaus-Uwe Panther and Günter Radden. Amsterdam: John Benjamins.

Newsom, Carol. 2007. "Spying out the Land: A Report from Genology." Pages 19-30 in *Bakhtin and Genre Theory in Biblical Studies*. Edited by Roland Boer. Atlanta: Society of Biblical Literature.

Niditch, Susan. 1996. *Oral World and Written World: Ancient Israelite Literature.* Louisville: Westminster John Knox.

———. (1987) 2000. *Underdogs and Tricksters: A Prelude to Biblical Folklore.* Urbana: University of Illinois Press.

Noegel, Scott B., and Gary Rendsburg. 2009. *Solomon's Vineyard: Literary and Linguistic Studies in the Song of Songs.* AIL 1. Atlanta: Society of Biblical Literature.

Nørgaard, Nina, Beatrix Busse, and Rocío Montoro. 2010. *Key Terms in Stylistics.* London: Bloomsbury.

Oegema, Gerbern. 2012. *Apocalyptic Interpretation of the Bible: Apocalypticism and Biblical Interpretation in Early Judaism, the Apostle Paul, the Historical Jesus and Their Reception History.* London/New York: T&T Clark.

Ortony, Andrew. 1993. *Metaphor and Thought.* 2nd ed. Cambridge: Cambridge University Press.

Paltridge, Brian. 1995. "Working with Genre: A Pragmatic Perspective." *Journal of Pragmatics* 24, no. 4: 393–406.

Panther, Klaus-Uwe, and Günter Radden, eds. 1999. *Metonymy in Language and Thought.* Amsterdam: John Benjamins.

Pavel, Thomas G. 1986. *Fictional Worlds.* London: Harvard University Press.

Petersen, Norman. 1978. *Literary Criticism for New Testament Critics.* Philadelphia: Fortress.

Polak, Frank. 2011. "Book, Scribe, and Bard." *Prooftexts* 31, no. 1/2: 118–40.

Porter, Stanley, ed. 2006. *Hearing the Old Testament in the New Testament.* Grand Rapids: Eerdmans.

Powell, Mark A. 2018. *Introducing the New Testament: A Historical, Literary, and Theological Survey.* 2nd ed. Grand Rapids: Baker Academic.

Punday, Daniel. 2005. "Creative Accounting: Role-playing Games, Possible-Worlds Theory, and the Agency of Imagination." *Poetics Today* 26, no. 1: 113–39.

Radden, Günter, and Zoltán Kövecses. 1999. "Towards a Theory of Metonymy." Pages 17–59 in *Metonymy in Language and Thought.* Edited by Klause-Uwe Panther and Günter Radden. Amsterdam: John Benjamins.

Ronen, Ruth. 1994. *Possible Worlds in Literary Theory.* Cambridge: Cambridge University Press.

Rosch, Eleanor. 1973a. "Natural Categories." *Cognitive Psychology* 4: 328–50.

———. 1973b. "On the Internal Structure of Perceptual and Semantic Categories." Pages 111–44 in *Cognitive Development and the Acquisition of Language.* Edited by Timothy E. Moore. New York: Academic Press.

——. 1975. "Cognitive Representations of Semantic Categories." *Journal of Experimental Psychology* 104: 192–233.

Rosch, Eleanor, and Carolyn Mervis. 1975. "Family Resemblances: Studies in the Structure of Categories." *Cognitive Psychology* 7: 573–605.

Rubba, Jo. 1996. "Alternate Grounds in the Interpretation of Deictic Expressions." Pages 227–61 in *Spaces, Worlds, and Grammar*. Edited by G. Fauconnier and E. Sweetser. Chicago: University of Chicago Press.

Rubin, Edgar. 1915. *Synsoplevede Figurer*. Copenhagen: Gyldendalsde Boghandel.

Ryan, Marie-Laure. 1991. *Possible Worlds, Artificial Intelligence and Narrative Theory*. Bloomington: Indiana University Press.

——. 1992. "Possible Worlds in Recent Literary Theory." *Style* 26, no. 4: 528–52.

——. 1998. "The Text as World versus the Text as Game: Possible Worlds Semantics and Postmodern Theory." *Journal of Literary Semantics* 27, no. 3: 137–63.

——. 2006. "From Parallel Universes to Possible Worlds: Ontological Pluralism in Physics, Narratology and Narrative." *Poetics Today* 27, no. 4: 633–741.

Sanders, José, and Gisela Redeker. 1996. "Perspective and the Representation of Speech and Thought in Narrative Discourse." Pages 290–317 in *Spaces, Worlds, and Grammar*. Edited by G. Fauconnier and E. Sweetser. Chicago: University of Chicago Press.

Sanford, Anthony J., and Simon C. Garrod. 1981. *Understanding Written Language: Comprehension Beyond the Sentence*. New York: Wiley & Sons.

Schank, Roger C. 1982. *Reading and Understanding: Teaching from the Perspective of Artificial Intelligence*. Hillsdale, NJ: Lawrence Erlbaum.

Schank, Roger C., and Robert Abelson. 1977. *Scripts, Plans, Goals and Understanding*. Hillsdale, NJ: Lawrence Erlbaum.

Segovia, Fernando F., and R. Sugirtharajah, eds. 2009. *A Postcolonial Commentary on the New Testament Writings*. London: T&T Clark.

Semino, Elena. 1997. *Language and World Creation in Poems and Other Texts*. London: Routledge.

——. 2005. "Possible Worlds: Stylistic Applications." Pages 777–82 in *Encyclopedia of Language and Linguistics*. Edited by K. Brown. Amsterdam: Elsevier Science.

Simpson, Paul. (2004) 2014. *Stylistics: A Resource Book for Students*. London/New York: Routledge.

Sinding, Michael. 2002. "After Definitions: Genre, Categories and Cognitive Science." *Genre* 35: 181–220.

Smith, Mark S. 2010. *The Priestly Vision of Genesis 1*. Minneapolis: Fortress.

Sternberg, Meir. 1985. *The Poetics of Biblical Narrative: Ideological Literature and the Drama of Reading*. Bloomington: Indiana University Press.

Stockwell, Peter. 2002. *Cognitive Poetics: An Introduction*. London: Routledge.

———. 2003. "Surreal Figures." Pages 13–25 in *Cognitive Poetics in Practice*. Edited by Joanna Gavins and Gerard Steen. London: Routledge.

———. 2009. *Texture: A Cognitive Aesthetics of Reading*. Edinburgh: Edinburgh University Press.

Swales, John. 1990. *Genre Analysis: English in Academic and Research Settings*. Cambridge: Cambridge University Press.

Swanson, James. 1997. Dictionary of Biblical Languages with Semantic Domains: Hebrew (Old Testament). Oak Harbor: Logos Research Systems, Inc.

Tannehill, Robert. 1986, 1990. *The Narrative Unity of Luke-Acts: A Literary Interpretation*. 2 vols. Philadelphia and Minneapolis: Fortress.

Taylor, John R. 1995. *Linguistic Categorization: Prototypes in Linguistic Theory*. 2nd ed. Oxford: Clarendon.

Taylor, Vincent. 1933. *The Formation of the Gospel Tradition: Eight Lectures*. London: Macmillan.

Trevisanato, Siro. 2005. *The Plagues of Egypt: Archaeology, History and Science Look at the Bible*. Piscataway, NJ: Gorgias.

Trible, Phyllis. 1994. *Rhetorical Criticism: Context, Method, and the Book of Jonah*. Minneapolis: Fortress.

Truszczyńska, Anna. 2002. *Conceptual Metonymy: The Problem of Boundaries in the Light of ICMs*. Berlin: de Gruyter.

Uhlenbruch, Frauke. 2015. *The Nowhere Bible: Utopia, Distopia, Science*. Berlin: de Gruyter.

Uhlenbruch, Frauke, Anna Angelini, and Anne-Sophie Augier, eds. 2017. *Not in the Spaces We Know: An Exploration of Science Fiction and the Bible*. Perspectives on Hebrew Scriptures and Its Contexts 24. Piscataway, NJ: Gorgias.

Van Hecke, Pierre, ed. 2005. *Metaphor in the Hebrew Bible*. Leuven: Peeters.

Van Hecke, Pierre, and Antje Labahn. 2010. *Metaphors in the Psalms*. [In English or German.] Bibliotheca Ephemeridum Theologicarum Lovaniensium. Leuven: Peeters.

Vermeulen, Karolien. 2017. "Save or Sack the City: The Fate of Jonah's Nineveh from a Spatial Perspective." *Journal for the Study of the Old Testament* 42, no. 2: 233–46.

Watson, Wilfred. 1984. *Classical Hebrew Poetry: A Guide to Its Techniques*. JSOTSup 26. Sheffield: JSOT Press.

Weiss, Meir. 1984. *The Bible from Within: The Method of Total Interpretation*. Jerusalem: Magnes.

Werth, Paul. 1994. "Extended Metaphor—a Text-World Account." *Language and Literature* 3: 79–103.

———. 1995. "How to Build a World (in a Lot Less that Six Days and Using Only What's in Your Head)." Pages 48–80 in *New Essays in Deixis: Discourse, Narrative, Literature*. Costerus 103. Edited by Keith Green. Amsterdam: Rodopi.

———. 1999. *Text Worlds: Representing Conceptual Space in Discourse*. London: Longman.

Whiteley, Sara. 2011. "Text World Theory, Real Readers and Emotional Responses to *The Remains of the Day*." *Language and Literature* 20, no. 1: 23–42.

Index of Subjects

acrostic structure, 17
actual worlds (AWs), 144, 145, 148
allusions, 100, 103–4
Alter, Robert, 2, 87, 99
alternate possible worlds (APWs), 145
analogical thinking, 107, 111
analogy, 89
ANGER IS HEAT conceptual metaphor, 121
animacy hierarchy, 109
antiparallelism, 46
antithesis, 15, 16–17
apocalyptic texts, 149
APWs (alternate possible worlds), 145
ark of the covenant, metonymies and, 119,
    126–28
artificial intelligence, 13, 86
Auerbach, Erich, 48
author-text connections, 100
AWs (actual worlds), 144, 145, 148

background knowledge: conceptual met-
    aphors and, 107, 113; discourse worlds
    and, 135, 139; encyclopedic, 9, 16, 94, 97,
    99, 107, 113, 161; mental spaces and, 94,
    97, 99; reading process and, 9, 16; text
    worlds and, 161
background style, 48
Bartlett, Frederic, 85–86
Berlin, Adele, 15
BETROTHAL schema, 87
Bible. See biblical poetry; biblical texts
Bible, reading of: cognitive stylistics and,
    2; conceptual blending and, 95–98; in

contemporary world, 138–39; discourse
    world and, 133, 138–39, 149–50; vs.
    general written texts, 64; genre and, 111,
    112; literary approaches and, 2; reader
    contexts/presuppositions and, 1, 2–3,
    112; reading processes and, 3; situations
    of speaking and, 57, 58; text consider-
    ations, 1. See also biblical studies
biblical poetry: metonymy in, 124–25;
    parallelism in, 26, 45, 48
biblical studies: background knowledge
    and, 161; categorization and prototypes
    in, 32–37; conceptual metaphors in,
    111–16; discourse worlds in, 136–41, 149–
    50; figure-ground in, 48–52; genre and,
    32–33, 111, 112; grammatical approaches
    in, 64, 68–76; imagery and, 111–12, 113,
    164; metonymies in, 124–28; perspective
    and deixis in, 55, 58–62; possible worlds
    in, 148–52; schemas and, 86–91; text
    worlds in, 157–66; words and meaning
    in, 9, 14–20
biblical texts: categorizing as literature,
    28–31, 32, 33, 34; coherence of, 126; de-
    scribing language of, 64; gaps in, 87–88;
    metaphor and metonymy in, 15–16;
    perspective and deixis in, 58, 60–61;
    possible worlds in, 148; readers' views
    of, 161; situations of speaking in, 58; as
    story, 148, 150; temple/cosmos forms
    and, 125; translation of (see translated
    texts/translation); universality of, 150.
    See also biblical poetry

189

scripts. *See* schemas

semantic domains: case study and examples, 11–12, 17–20; defined, 11; history of, 13–14; vs. lexical domains, 11; metaphor and, 11, 17; numbering of, 13–14; parallelism and, 16–17, 18–19

semiotic triangle, 122

senses, human, 66

Short, Mick, 161

simile, 15, 106

SIN AND REPENTANCE schema, 89

single metaphors, 112, 113

situation of speaking, 55–57, 58–59

Sitz im Leben, 137

SLAVERY schema, 82

slots, 84

SOCIETY IS A PLANT metaphor, 109–10, 168

Song of Songs (case study), 139–41

source domains: conceptual metaphors and, 106, 107, 108, 109, 110, 114–15; text worlds and, 163, 164

SOURCE-PATH-GOAL SCHEMA, 66, 67–68, 73, 76, 107

space, 61–62, 68

Spaces, Worlds, and Grammar (Fauconnier and Sweetser), 98

speech, reported, 58–59, 159

SPEECH schema, 83–84

speech space/world, 113, 114–15, 163

split discourse world, 134, 138–39, 140

Sternberg, Meir, 99

Stockwell, Peter, 42

story elements, 26, 88–89

Strong's Concordance, 10–11

structural details, 16. *See also* parallelism

style, textual, 48

stylistic figures, 49

stylistics, 2–3

subworlds, 156, 159, 165–66

SUPPER schema, 86–87

Swanson, James, 14

Sweetser, Eve, 98

synecdoche, 124

synonymy, 15, 16–17

synthesis, 15

TABERNACLE FOR TEMPLE metonymy, 125

target domains: conceptual metaphors and, 106, 107, 108, 109, 110, 114–15, 164; text worlds and, 163, 164

target entity, 119

technology, 13

temple, form of, 125

text drivenness, principle of, 136

text schemas, 85

textual actual world (TAW), 144–45, 147–48

text worlds: background knowledge and, 161; in biblical studies, 161–62; case study and examples, 157–60, 162–67; conceptual blending and, 156, 164; conceptual metaphor and, 113, 164; defined, 155; deixis and, 58; double vision and, 164, 166; elements of, 139–40; language and, 162; mental spaces and, 160; reader participation with, 155–56; situations of speaking and, 58. *See also* Text World Theory

Text Worlds (Werth), 161

Text World Theory, 136–37, 160–61

Text World Theory (Gavins), 161

things (grammatical category), 65, 69, 76

time, 68

time deixis, 61

top-down process, 82, 88

translated texts/translation: biblical interpretation and, 74; cognitive grammar and, 64, 68, 74; lack of one-to-one equivalence in, 9, 14, 74; "little words" in, 72; reader preunderstandings/presuppositions and, 16; translation approaches, 14; words in context and, 14

tricksters, 150

Turner, Mark, 98

type-scenes, 87

unmarked language, 43, 43n2, 45

usage event, 69, 71

Valley of Dry Bones (case study), 151–52

vehicle entity, 119

verbs: in cognitive grammar, 65, 67–68,

Index of Scripture